Garden Ideas

❧ CREATIVE DESIGN SOLUTIONS ❧

WARREN SCHULTZ   CAROL SPIER

MetroBooks

MetroBooks

An Imprint of Friedman/Fairfax Publishers

Library of Congress Cataloging-in-Publication Data available upon request.

ISBN 1-56799-493-8

Editor: Kelly Matthews
Art Directors: Jeff Batzli and Lynne Yeamans
Designer: Stan Stanski
Layout: Philip Travisano
Photography Editor: Susan Mettler
Photography Director: Christopher C. Bain
Production Manager: Camille Lee

Color separations by Fine Arts Repro House Co., Ltd.
Printed in China by Leefung-Asco Printers Ltd.

10 9 8 7 6 5 4 3 2

For bulk purchases and special sales, please contact:
Friedman/Fairfax Publishers
Attention: Sales Department
15 West 26th Street
New York, NY 10010
212/685-6610 FAX 212/685-1307

Visit our website:
http://www.metrobooks.com

Table of Contents

Introduction
CREATING THE GARDEN OF YOUR DREAMS
6

INTRODUCTION
Creating the Garden of Your Dreams

What is it that makes certain gardens truly extraordinary? There is no denying that some gardens go beyond merely pretty and live forever in memory as nothing short of breathtaking. Would you be surprised to learn that countless stunning garden effects are well within your grasp? Whatever sort of garden you have (or hope to have), be it rolling acres in a country setting or a jewel box in the city, you can create a gorgeous garden paradise more easily than you might ever have dreamed. You don't need a great deal of experience or money; you can achieve an extraordinary garden even if you don't fancy yourself a natural designer.

Believe it or not, it comes down to this: the loveliest gardens are those that make the most of their given situation. This is achieved in three ways. First, be true to the site by working with nature, rather than battling it. If good, direct sun exposure is in scarce supply, planting a garden of sun worshipers is sure to be disappointing. Make the most of your site and situation. Second, once your overall garden plan has had a chance to get started, consider how you can embellish your theme. Make the most of every corner and vista; ornamentation is virtually always possible. Finally, remember that you can change any effect that falls short of your hopes. Give plants the chance to perform, but if the result isn't pleasing, make the most of your time by calling a halt to your experiment and trying something else.

In the pages that follow, you'll be delighted by hundreds upon hundreds of inspiring ideas for adding romance and unique style to your garden. Garden ornamentation is one of the easiest—and most effective—ways to make the most of your garden. Special touches make even the smallest patch of ground a thing of beauty. Consider adding water features to your garden, including naturalistic or formal pools, marsh beds, waterfalls, and streams—even bridges and walkways, if only for sheer ornamental pleasure. Nothing is as calming as the sound of moving water in the garden, and you can choose from scores of stunning designs. Every garden can be enhanced by water, and wetland and water plants add handsome variety and a touch of the exotic.

It's a simple matter to succeed when you put the right plant in the right place, and here you will find wonderful suggestions for plants and plant combinations for those tricky shade and marsh locations. Whether you want the impressionist effect of bright colors in all hues and heights, or luxuriant sweeps of lush emerald ground cover, turn here for suggestions. Shade offers the gardener the greatest challenge. Yet when shade-loving plants are happily sited, few can surpass them for sheer beauty and vigor. And because there are varying degrees of shade, you'll find recommendations for annuals, perennials, ground covers, and shrubs for light, medium, dark, and even dappled shade. You will see how to turn areas of deepest shade literally into the highlights of your garden.

Looking to add dimension to your garden? Consider what arbors and trellises have to offer—the romance of "vertical gardening." Vines and creepers provide cooling shade or brilliant blooms, often perfuming the air with their fragrance. Because they are elevated, they may thrive where other plants couldn't hope to grow. A pretty frame can support masses of gorgeous flowers above an already full bed. Choose from a wide array of climbers that can provide you with great bowlfuls of flowers all summer long. You may love the informality of a rustic wooden arbor or the Victorian charm of a wrought-iron archway, and such ornaments can serve as impressive focal points in your garden scheme.

We may think of window boxes as the very essence of summer. Here, though, you will learn how to extend the enjoyment of your pretty window boxes from early spring right through autumn. And as popular as these planters are for adding splashes of seasonal color, they can be so much more. Use them to bring the outdoors inside; the planting you choose frames your view from the window. Try an herb garden in miniature! Look here for a wealth of planting suggestions for gaily colored mixes, bold monochromatic plantings, and color schemes in tones that range from cool to fiery. With advice on just the right plants for your sun exposure, you can create a thriving window garden to express whatever effect you desire, from stately to whimsical. Arrange plants to spill gracefully over the sides or grow upward in imitation of a garden border; the choice is up to you.

Generously photographed in everything from tailored boxes with molding or unfinished wood silvered by weather to baskets and hollow logs, even humble windowsills turn glamorous in these pages.

What will make your garden unforgettable? Will it be a favorite view framed by a fragrant, bloom-covered arching trellis? A collection of country garden seats beneath cheerful window boxes? A wandering alley bordered by the cool colors of shade-loving shrubs in full flower? The charm is in the personal touches you add. Let the hundreds of spectacularly photographed suggestions here guide you to a more beautiful garden.

—Rebecca W. Atwater Briccetti

ABOVE: Whatever your site and situation, there are countless plants that will enrich your landscape. Here, pale yellow water lilies grace the smooth surface of a pool; along its banks grow marsh-loving ornamental grasses, black-eyed Susans, and drifts of wildflowers.

Part One
WINDOW BOXES

CAROL SPIER

INTRODUCTION

*W*indow boxes are like grace notes, accenting a composition of landscape and architecture with charm, whimsy, dignity, or color. Small gardens set above the ground, window boxes trim and finish a facade the way a bouquet or a dried flower arrangement finishes a room's decor, enhancing its style and creating or emphasizing a mood by their shape, color, and demeanor. In addition, they bring a bit of prettily tilled soil within reach of inhabitants, complete with bees, butterflies, occasional birds, and the thrills and vagaries of seasonal gardening that simply are not offered by house plants.

In cities or in towns where the homes are built right up against the sidewalks, window boxes may offer residents their only opportunity to have a garden, and they also serve to soften the appearance of the landscape. In more rural settings, window boxes provide a link between lawn and home, complementing and extending the gardens below. Boxes can be sophisticated or rustic in design, permanently or seasonally displayed, formally or informally planted. You can grow flowers, small shrubs, vines, and herbs in window boxes, depending upon the seasonal effects desired, location of the box, and climate in which you live. In addition, your plantings may be annual or perennial.

Window boxes from many different settings have been gathered here. Some are straightforward, others are fanciful, adorning a home such as yours or such as you might dream of. You may choose to interpret some boxes for your own landscape, while others may not be appropriate, but all should please on the merit of their existing charm.

INTEGRATING WINDOW BOXES WITH YOUR LANDSCAPE

When you add a window box to your home, it should be in keeping with the style of the facade and landscape. Window boxes are usually charming, but there is a fine line between charming and trite, and not every dwelling will be enhanced by elevated boxes of blooms. As you consider whether to add window boxes and what

type of box and plantings to use, look around your neighborhood and in architecture, gardening, and travel books and magazines for ideas that please you, and note as well any boxes that seem inappropriate in their settings. You want your box to enhance your home, not to gussy it up, so balance the style and size of the box and the shape and color of the plantings with the style, color, and proportions of your home and landscape.

ABOVE: This Federal-style home sits just a step away from the sidewalk, and the tiny yard permits just a bit of foundation planting. The small green window boxes continue the orderly trim of the shutters. Filled with trailing ivy and lantana, they give a soft finish to this very proper dwelling.

OPPOSITE: There is no room for front-yard gardens on this block of town houses, but each sill holds a window box that softens the formal expanse of brick. The quiet, monochromatic plantings are in keeping with the elegant architecture but bring a humanizing hint of domesticity to the urban setting. Even a small touch of gardening seems to give a neighborhood a residential character; window boxes placed on city shops, as well as homes, will appear welcoming to passersby.

LEFT: In older European cities, it is quite common to find stone houses built one against the other along narrow streets. Rarely blessed with front gardens, they can present a cold and rather gloomy face when left unadorned—which is not very often. One sees lovingly tended window boxes bringing color and life to nearly every sill for as much of the year as weather permits.

BELOW: In a suburban setting, window boxes are likely to be combined with other landscape details. This Tudor-style home sits comfortably among mature trees and shrubs and in spring is surrounded by lavish blooms. The window boxes soften the dark facade and sharply contrasting white trim and carry the spring flowers charmingly but discreetly up to every floor.

ABOVE: Dozens of red geraniums provide the only note of color found on the facade of this large and handsome Colonial Revival house, with dozens more lining the walkway. Such an unbroken expanse of white adds a touch of severity to the formality of the architecture; the regularly repeating red offers a bit of wanted but appropriately controlled relief.

ABOVE: The sun beats unrelentingly on the stone houses at the top of this ancient hillside village in rural France. Although the houses are closely spaced and it is too steep to garden here easily, the residents managed to establish a small plot of flowers and train a great grapevine over the streetside doorway. The fanciful ironwork is bravely lighthearted against the heavy stone; the lovely curved balconet, never intended for human occupation, makes a luxurious window box.

OPPOSITE: This Tudor-style village home rises above a narrow, cobbled courtyard that offers little space for gardening. This is a sunny spot, however, and the hard aspect of stone and stucco is cheered by the sprightly dahlias, exuberantly climbing roses, and boxes of cascading geraniums.

RIGHT: The front of this small country home is shaded by a porch that keeps direct light from the windows, so a window box fills the bay over the porch rail instead. The walkway up to the steps is dotted with small planters; the vines trailing from the box carry the eye from one charming mound of blooms to the next.

ABOVE: In an open rural setting where the first view of a building may be from afar, the window plantings must be bold enough to hold their own against the architecture. The window bays of the porch along the front of this old Alpine granary are filled with boxes of red ivy geraniums, each spilling a strong band of color over the railings.

LEFT: This rustic shed has grown into its setting over time, weathering to the wonderful muted gray that is the perfect backdrop for pink and purple blossoms waving amid soft greenery. The box that sits unpretentiously below the primitive windows echoes their strong horizontal line with another in pink and green.

ABOVE: If your windows are long and close to the ground, then your window box plantings can relate directly to whatever is growing below. The brick terrace backing this home is lined with the variously colored and textured greenery of potted herbs; the rosemary in the box in the window reaches down to them. Imagine the fragrance when this window is raised.

RIGHT: Although we tend to think of window boxes as ornaments for the front of a house, they can just as happily trim the back, and if the back gardens are extensive, boxes can carry the plantings gaily up the wall. Here, a marvelous terrace is framed on three sides by a showy English border, and the back of the house acts as the fourth with the window boxes and hanging baskets integrating the wall with its landscape.

ABOVE: Great masses of real blooms dance before trompe l'oeil woodwork and frescoed scenes from a passion play in this special setting. Even though you might shy away from the pictorials, the painted trim is not inappropriate—or unattainable—for a stucco building, and the window boxes simply enhance the illusion.

OPPOSITE: Admittedly, a house edged by water may not be the norm, but if this happens to be your situation, take advantage of the water's reflective surface; any detail that is charming once is doubly so when mirrored. Here, lush geraniums tumble out of three windows twice.

WHAT KIND OF BOX?

The look of the box you place in your window may be as important to you as the plantings that will fill it, or if your plan calls for it to be obscured by the vegetation, your only concerns may be price, weight, and durability. When you shop for window boxes, you will see that they are available to suit every fanciful whim and fit any sophisticated style of architecture—for a price. There are, however, many good-looking and possibly more durable models to be found in most hardware or gardening supply stores. If you are handy with a hammer and saw, you can easily build your own.

Keep in mind that window boxes must have good drainage to prevent rot and that they will be heavy when filled, so be sure to consider how you will secure them to your house. Although terra-cotta and wood are very attractive, they do not always survive extremes of damp or temperature, so if you plan to leave your boxes out year-round, be sure they are fabricated and finished appropriately for your climate. You may find that a box made of metal, fiberglass, or a polymer will be a better investment, and if interestingly painted or when viewed from the street, you may not be able to tell the difference.

ABOVE: If copper is left to weather naturally, it takes on a wonderful verdigris patina that is complementary to most foliage and flowers. This look of natural antiquity is presently in vogue, and if you can't manage a real copper box, you might buy a do-it-yourself verdigris faux-finishing kit that will simulate the look on a number of other materials.

OPPOSITE: It is difficult to say whether it is the pressed-metal window boxes or drainpipe that is most charming here; certainly one complements the other—and the masonry—beautifully. The boxes are supported by sturdy but elegant brackets.

ABOVE: Paint can really dress up a wood box and help it to weather the elements. The color of course is a matter of personal preference; here, brilliant red makes a bold accent out of a humble box, setting off fuchsia and white blooms with aplomb.

OPPOSITE: Unfinished wood lends rustic charm to a window box. Here, five weathered boards were crudely banged together; this box makes no pretense to elegance but is very charming in this setting.

OPPOSITE: On this traditional clapboard home neat bands of contrasting molding finish a tailored window box with just enough sophistication to suit its surprisingly ornate supporting bracket. The cool and unified paint scheme keeps the effect low-key as foliage, living and ornamental, casts graceful shadows.

ABOVE: Spanning the length of a large picture window, this classic square-edged wooden box is so long that it needs to rest on sturdy brackets. There is nothing fancy about a homemade box such as this, but once painted to match the window trim and filled with robust plants, it is unobtrusive, serviceable, and good-looking.

OPPOSITE: A hollowed log makes a witty and perfectly appropriate window box to attach to a log house. The more this one weathers, the more it will have the aspect of an overgrown fallen branch in a woodland glade.

ABOVE: Flat-backed baskets make charming hanging planters—or window boxes. They bring an exuberant, informal sparkle to this rustic building. Baskets are easy to find, hang, and plant, but as they age, check the bottoms to make sure they are not rotting out.

ABOVE: Absorbent terra-cotta is of course an ideal material for flowerpots or any other sort of planter. Not all terra-cotta can withstand freezing, but otherwise, it is durable and weathers well. Terra-cotta is available in myriad styles—from the simple troughs sitting on this stone sill to more intricate and fancifully cast pieces—and its warm, rusty tones evoke visions of the Mediterranean wherever it is found.

OPPOSITE: Cast stone is a traditional material for all sorts of garden ornament; it weathers well and complements most foliage. It is durable and fairly inexpensive, but heavy. Boxes of cast stone may be very simple or quite elegant. This lovely footed box brings a wonderful element of profusion to its overgrown setting.

ABOVE: In some forms of architecture, brackets, often made of ornamental ironwork, extend above the sill to form a window guard called a balconet. A balconet can be fanciful or elaborate, like the semi-circular one on page 11, or simple. The one surrounding this box is just a simple fence of uprights that breaks up the long plain surface of the terra-cotta. This locale is so overgrown with ivy that anything more elaborate would be lost.

LEFT: Window boxes are sometimes partially obscured by brackets that form a cage around them. When this is the case, the brackets are usually more interesting to look at than the boxes, which should be plain so as not to interfere. This simple green box sits on a shelf that is fenced with miniature pickets; the ivy geraniums tumbling over them look like rambling roses along a full-size garden fence.

ABOVE: If your windows are especially pretty or interestingly trimmed, an ornate window box might detract from their inherent charms. To keep the focus on the architecture, choose a plain box and let the plantings obscure it with a soft, colorful accent—as does the froth of ivy geraniums at this scroll-embellished corner.

ABOVE: A row of pots lining a sill gives an effect similar to that of a true window box, and has the advantage of easy transfer indoors when the season turns. Oddly assorted pots lend a casual ambiance, so choose matching ones if a formal display is preferred—and be sure your sill is deep and level enough to house them securely.

A Matter of Style

As with any other form of gardening, the design of a window garden may be formal or informal, and there are a number of factors that determine which look is appropriate to a particular location. Often, the architectural style of the building will set the tone, indicating the style of both box and plantings, but just as often, the whim of the gardener can steer the choice, creating a soft and naturalistic box for a row house or one that observes some formal rule of color or shape for a cottage. As you decide, consider how the different looks would complement your home and what sort of mood they would convey. If you feel unsure of your design talents, it is never wrong to stick with the traditional, but remember that window boxes are small, and unless you are installing a lot of them, you can experiment with different looks without making a huge investment of time or money. In addition, there are times when the distinction between formal and informal becomes purely subjective, so concentrate on creating a box that pleases you, trust your instincts, remember that a formal garden design is only as good as maintenance keeps it, and have fun.

FORMAL PLANTINGS AND BOXES

Formal window boxes are most often seen on formal buildings in urban locations. The boxes can be plain or embellished with architectural details—perhaps repeating a motif seen elsewhere on the building—and they can be made of almost any material with a plain or natural finish or perhaps a fancy painted one. While they ought not to be not folkloric or rustic, they might have an antique patina or a shadow of moss.

Formal plantings follow a regular, orderly plan, usually one that relies upon symmetry of shape and color to provide balance. It is not so much the type of plants chosen as the way they are arranged that gives a box a formal demeanor, although you are more likely to use small shrubs or topiaries in a formal rather than an informal box, and some climbing and cascading plants have an exuberance that sets an informal tone.

ABOVE: The rim of this stone balconet is lined with plain boxes, each of which holds two cyclamens with elegant blooms erect above mounding foliage. The simple, regularly punctuated bands made by boxes, leaves, and flowers provide just the right accent for the complex facade behind them; the lobed blossoms pay a nice compliment to the trefoil arches topping the windows.

OPPOSITE: A carved and painted peacock, a formal bird if ever there was one, stands in proud display on this otherwise simple box. Three regularly spaced mounds of ivy have been trained over wire forms. The box is very subtle in this ivy-covered setting, with an aura of the antique and mysterious that is often found in old, shadowy formal gardens.

ABOVE: Although summery massed plantings soften the front of this London town house, they are arranged in an orderly manner; in the basket and each box, lobelia cascades below a mound of geraniums and petunias—blue below red and pink.

OPPOSITE: A plain white box continues the clean graphic effect of the pedimented window trim on this stuccoed building. Alyssum spills demurely over the front of the box; bright red geraniums appear dignified against their deep and variegated leaves in this pristine, controlled setting.

RIGHT: A massive building such as this stone retreat calls for a substantial rather than delicate window garden. Here, a great band of coleus rounds out the sill below the middle window bay and the vinca trails elegantly down to meet the ground cover. Coleus, which derives its quiet beauty from variegated leaves rather than showy blooms, is an apt choice to set in this dappled light against the strong texture of the stonework.

INFORMAL PLANTINGS AND BOXES

Informal window boxes lack the self-conscious control of formal ones—which doesn't mean that thought isn't given to their composition. They often contain a disparate assortment of plants that mingle with seeming abandon as they trail, climb, or spring from the box, but to be successful, the colors and shapes must be assembled with an eye toward harmony.

Informal window gardens can be planted in plain boxes or in rustic or earthy ones. An informal window garden may share the exuberance of a cottage garden, overflowing its plot so the box hardly shows, or its design may take its cue from the demeanor and material of the container, but it is unlikely that you would choose an elegantly ornamented box for a naturalistic planting.

OPPOSITE: Although most urban row houses have facades that are somewhat formal, they do not dictate the creation of formal window boxes unless they are built in a particularly mannered style. In fact, informal window gardens can soften the aspect of a town house. Here, unmatched gardens send sprightly horizontal bands of color splashing across a brick facade; though unalike, they are united by their shared overall shape and use of white and warm-colored blooms and trailing greens.

ABOVE: You need not mix a lot of plants or colors to create an informal window garden. Bright blue trim gives this small double window an unusual importance that is complemented by small, intensely yellow marigold blossoms peeking casually through a mass of feathery, dark green ferns.

ABOVE: In this wildly happy spot, it seems that a bit of everything that loves the sun has been gathered into one box. This garden works because the colors are well balanced and none of the plants has blooms or leaves that are overly large.

RIGHT: Snapdragons might seem an unusual choice to fill a window box, but they appear to be wonderfully happy here, giving this box the feeling of a full-blown country border. Taller stalks stand at lively attention to the sun above a mass of shorter snaps and violas; this mingling of intense colors is particularly pleasing.

OPPOSITE: Although the palette chosen for this rather sweet and maidenly planting is limited to pink, purple, and green and the arrangement is fairly orderly, the ivy trailing in and out of the dancing and cascading flowers breaks up the composition and gives it an informal air.

ABOVE: This window box has been filled with an informal gathering consisting mainly of herbs. The collection makes a wonderfully textured and fragrant mound of variegated green, and the effect is delicate and private rather than showy.

ABOVE: Here, lavish use of overflowing window boxes set amid rivulets of climbing ivy softens an otherwise severe facade. The composition of color and plants is repetitive, but the mood is carefree, not controlled.

OPPOSITE: If your home is sufficiently rustic or archaic in mood to support an abundance of exuberant window plantings, then let your green thumb run riot. Here, terra-cotta boxes and pots frame windows and doors, spilling jewel-toned blossoms in cheerful abandon over the old stones.

A Matter of Color

Color may be the single most important design element in your window box. From a distance, you will notice the color of a composition before you are able to perceive anything else about it, and you will know at once if it is bright or pastel, cheery or demure, and probably whether it is a mass of a single color or a mix of many. You will also be able to tell immediately if the colors used in a window box flatter or clash with the facade they trim.

Color can suggest mood and attitude. The way colors are arranged can emphasize or create movement within a window box design. As you select your plants, think not only of their color and whether the blooms punctuate or obscure the foliage, but also of their growth habits—upright, mounding, cascading, or trailing—and of how you can work these elements together. Consider the length of a plant's blooming season, and whether you want to redo your box as the seasons change, or whether you would prefer something that will last from late spring to early autumn. Decide also if you would like a monochromatic box or one that is multicolored; either can be formal or informal, subtle or strong, and both are lovely.

MONOCHROMATIC PLANTINGS

Whether they are formal or informal in shape, subtle or dynamic in color, monochromatic window box plantings will generally provide an uncomplicated accent of color to a facade. By using only one color or one color plus foliage, you automatically simplify the number of elements that a viewer must absorb and your box will have a more graphic impact when seen from a distance. Up close you will be able to appreciate all the subtle variations of texture that might be lost in a melange of color.

ABOVE: The ivy geraniums twining through this wrought-iron window guard share its red color, and together they make a unified and delicate contrast to the white wall and lace curtain.

OPPOSITE: Red window trim brightens and punctuates the facade of this log home. By matching the geraniums to the paint, the impact of the box merges with that of the window as a single strong and graphic element.

ABOVE: Although not truly monochromatic, these boxes produce the initial impression of a great cascade of greenery softening the facade of the clapboard home they adorn. The foliage is far more important to this design than the flowers, and because the blooms match the shutters, they do not intrude upon the overall effect.

LEFT: Three ivy geraniums spill pink blossoms out of this large window. Because the geraniums are of the same type, the slight variation in their color does not distract from the impression of a pink cascade; it just adds a bit of life to the large display.

ABOVE: A boxful of herbs will always provide a study in subtle variations. Without the distraction of showy blossoms, one can take in all the curls, cuts, and velvets of the leaves, and the mounds, umbrellas, and cascades of the growth habits. A box as discreet as this would not have much impact when seen from halfway down the block, but it would add a graceful accent to a terrace or be a welcome addition on a kitchen sill.

ABOVE: A mass of wonderful egg-yolk yellow cheers this white box and window, picking up the warmth of the sunny brick wall around it. The choice of foliage is most appropriate, the yellow edge of the ivy complementing the rich blooms. (Scotch broom and chrysanthemums do not share a natural blooming season, so a box that duplicates this exactly must be intended for short-term display.)

ABOVE: A simple drape of deep blue lobelia is the perfect foil to the wonderful turquoise that colors real and trompe l'oeil trim on this California home. This window is so complex that it has no need for an elaborately designed planting; the choice made here is inspired.

OPPOSITE: Here, a lovely arrangement in white relies upon the differing sizes and textures of blooms for articulation. The white all but obscures the foliage, and the white-edged vinca continues the theme as it trails down the facade.

MULTICOLORED PLANTINGS

When you arrange a planting of colorful flowers, you have one of the most lavish paint boxes imaginable to work from. With the myriad hues and values available, you can create a window box that is impressionistic, graphic, vibrant, or controlled. You can select a palette that is warm or cool, made of complementary colors (from opposite sides of the color wheel) or analogous ones (neighbors on the color wheel). You can arrange a composition in which the colors follow some clearly marked pattern or mix them all together in a random manner.

The growing habits of the plants you choose will affect the way your arrangement matures, so think not only of the colors of the blossoms but of whether they appear on upright or trailing stems, whether they obscure their foliage or punctuate it, and whether a single specimen or a mass is needed to be most effective in your design. And don't neglect foliage plants; the greens available may be pure or tinted with yellow, gray, blue, and even red tones that complement or contrast different flowers in different ways.

ABOVE LEFT: The colors in this intimate window box were chosen for the rich value of their deep tones—egg-yolk yellow, purple, dark blue and green, and a bit of red—and arranged in small masses. Note how diminutive white and yellow blooms punctuate the composition.

ABOVE RIGHT: This half-round basket holds a sweet display of spring blooms—pansies, violas, impatiens, lobelia. All are delicately formed and richly hued, with just enough of each to make a pretty bouquet.

OPPOSITE: The window box taken, perhaps, to an extreme—but how magnificent. Here, tiers of hanging flower pots supplement the basic box and overflow with a melange of color and texture. This composition is not as haphazard as it first appears—it was planted symmetrically and arranged with an eye to texture and growth habit as well as color. As it matured, a marvelous mingling occurred.

ABOVE: Jewel-tone nasturtiums compose their own carefree display. Plant seeds from an assorted pack and you are guaranteed a balanced arrangement, complex and harmonious—and charming enough be the sole choice for a small box. Different types of nasturtiums trail, climb, or mound and have green or variegated foliage, so choose one that will grow as you desire.

OPPOSITE: Pink, purply blue, and white are the only colors set against the green in this small box. Blossoms of a different size and character were chosen for each color; the effect is simple and unpretentious but controlled.

OPPOSITE: A limited palette has been planted in controlled tiers of alternating color in this box, allowing the eye to appreciate each variation in texture and shape. These colors would be just as harmonious if arranged in a looser manner, but the mood of the composition would be quite different.

ABOVE: Daisies and lobelia are profuse bloomers with feathery foliage and gently disordered growth habits; here, they mingle charmingly in an impressionistic froth that softens the more intense pink of the geraniums that share the box.

A Matter of Location

Light and climate, two influential conditions that are beyond the control of the gardener, affect the contents of window boxes as much as they do larger in-ground gardens. There are plants that thrive in shady conditions, others that require long hours of sun, and some that will thrive in either as long as they are properly watered. In the right climate, cacti, succulents, orchids, or bromeliads can be as wonderful in a window box as the more usual geraniums or impatiens. And no matter what the growing conditions, bright colors will make a location seem warmer, pale ones cooler. If you are in doubt as to what will be best for your location, consult a local nursery.

LEFT: This shady window is itself shaded by a curtain of pink, purple, and green. The window box is blanketed with impatiens but also holds climbing blooms, which twine toward the hanging basket of elegant fuchsia. Note how the medium-pink tones glow against the green in the dappled light.

OPPOSITE: Although impatiens are most often seen in shade or filtered light, they will survive in fairly sunny conditions as long as they don't get too hot and dry. Here, they mound prettily over a rustic box on a weathered board-and-batten wall.

ABOVE: As impatiens are a standard choice for shady windowsills, geraniums are ubiquitous on sunny ones. Luckily, they come in many shades of red, orange, and pink—and white as well—with upright or trailing growth habits and smooth, lobed, bright, and variegated leaves, so they offer lots of cheery possibility. Here, ivy geraniums spill out of casement windows onto an ivy-covered wall—a typical sight all over France.

LEFT: Begonias thrive in full sun or partial shade; here, their warm tones brighten a cool window.

ABOVE: A window in a wall bleached out by constant sun needs a box filled with strong colors that can stand up to the hot light. Lipstick, fuchsia, and egg yolk–colored flowers accent rich green foliage and hold their own on this bright sill.

OPPOSITE: Petunias are a classic choice for sunny window boxes. They come in white and almost any imaginable shade of red or blue; some varieties have striped petals that lend them a carnival air. Here, a soft melange of pink, lavender, and white blooms tumbles over an elegantly detailed box; the soft colors against the gray wood have a cooling effect on the sunny facade.

A MATTER OF SEASON

*Y*ou may or may not wish to acknowledge the changing seasons in your window box designs—many gardeners prefer to wait till the spring sun warms enough to presage summer and then create a box that will last until frost. Of course, you may be one of those who simply cannot resist the first primroses and pansies and is prepared to trade them for something more heat-tolerant later in the season. And when frost knocks out your summer blooms, you may find a barren box unbearable and fill it with dwarf evergreens or a dried arrangement.

The climate in which you live and the overall nature of your landscaping will no doubt influence your choice of seasonal schemes. Some colors are naturally associated with certain seasons—pastels for spring, brights for summer, rich rusty tones for autumn, and evergreens for winter—but these associations are hardly rules. Springtime's yellows are as intense as any you might find in summer's flower beds, and there are as many pale pinks to be found in summer's sun and shade as there are in spring's first buds; so think first of the type of plants you wish to use, and then select colors that suit your mood.

ABOVE: Pansies and violas are full of simple springtime cheer—their determined little faces always indicate that warmer weather is on the way. This is a lovely use of tonal color in a mellow setting.

OPPOSITE: Fragrant, starry-eyed primroses make an appearance in hothouses soon after the winter solstice and are among the first flowers offered by nurseries in the spring. They are hardy outdoors year-round where winters are mild and will sometimes surprise you with blooms peeking up from leaf mulch and light snow. Planted with amaryllis in these beautiful cast-stone troughs, they offer a bright encouragement to springtime.

ABOVE: Even a quick glance at this joyful mound of hot colors lets you know—or feel—that high summer is at hand. Note that this lively arrangement has lots of red—and not a geranium in sight.

OPPOSITE: The flowers chosen for this small box will bloom from late spring until frost. This is a charming composition of contrasts—and contains a numerous variety for such a tiny spot.

ABOVE: Here is a very pretty, and slightly unexpected, arrangement of summer's classic blooms. The pendant fuchsia carry the hot red of the geraniums gaily down into the cooler purple of the lobelia, while the pale pink geraniums complement the stone panel below the box and pick up the light tone that accents the red and purple cascade.

ABOVE: As the days cool toward autumn, our eyes yearn for some of the same warmth our bodies find in sweaters and scarves. Chrysanthemums offer a soft and velvety blanket of russet tones; here, a band of small plants in full bloom nestles cozily against a windowsill.

OPPOSITE: A building with an impressive facade can carry a grand display of autumn color. Here, a magnificent blanket of gold and white chrysanthemums takes in the air on a balcony railing fronting stately French doors; like us, they seem to enjoy basking in the last warm light of the year.

ABOVE: Although the season for outdoor flowers passes with the coming of winter, there is no reason to let your window boxes stand naked and forlorn against the cold weather. Try planting small evergreens—perhaps topiary trained—in your boxes, or fill them with seasonal arrangements of dried naturals, cut greens, or a combination, as shown here. Remember that cut or dried arrangements need as much care—or more—as living ones, so don't abandon them to wind and snow, and don't let holiday displays outstay their purpose.

Plants for Window Boxes

blue daisy (*Felicia amelloides*)
blue cupflower (*Nierembergia caerulia*)
Boston fern (*Nephrolepis exaltata* 'Bostoniensis')
browallia (*Browallia* spp.)
chamomile (*Anthemis* spp.)
columbine (*Aquilegia vulgaris*)
common heliotrope (*Heliotropium arborescens*)
cornflower (*Centaura* spp.)
creeping jenny (*Lysimachia nummularia aurea*)
daisy (*Bellis* spp.)
dwarf lavender (*Lavandula* 'Hidcote')
dwarf mallow (*Malva* spp., dwarf cultivars)
feather duster plant (*Celosia amaranthaceae*)
geranium (*Pelargonium* × *hortorum*)
grape hyacinth (*Muscari* spp.)
impatiens (*Impatiens wallerana*)
licorice plant (*Helichrysum peliolatum*)
lobelia (*Lobelia erinus*)
monkey flower (*Mimulus* spp.)
periwinkle (*Catharanthus roseus*)
petunia (*Petunia* × *hybrida*)
pot marigold (*Calendula officinalis*)
snow in summer (*Cerastium tomentosum*)
sweet alyssum (*Lobularia maritima*)
tuberous begonia (*Begonia* × *tuberhybrida*)
wax begonia (*Begonia* × *semperflorens*)

A Container Garden

Plant List
(number of plants needed in parentheses)

HANGING BASKETS
1. Fuschia, *Fuschia* × *hybrida* 'Swingtime' (2)
2. Impatiens, *Impatiens wallerana* 'Futura Red' (3 baskets with 3 plants each)
3. Dallas fern, *Nephrolepis exaltata* 'Dallas' (1)
4. Tomato, *Lycopersicon lycopersicum* 'Basket King' (1)

BENCH PLANTERS
1. Variegated annual vinca, *Vinca major* 'Variegata' (7)
2. Mealy-cup sage, *Salvia farinacea* 'Victoria' (5)

3. French marigold, *Tagetes patula* 'Queen Sophia' (9)
4. French marigold, *Tagetes patula* 'Janie Flame' (10)
5. Tomato, *Lycopersicon lycopersicum* 'Pixie II' (5)
6. Sweet pepper, *Capsicum annuum* 'Park's Pot' (5)
7. Common garden petunia, *Petunia* × *hybrida* 'Yellow Magic' (8)
8. Garden nasturtium, *Tropaeolum majus* 'Whirlybird Mixed' (14)
9. Ornamental pepper, *Capsicum annuum* 'Holiday Flame' (11)
10. Italian bellflower, *Campanula isophylla* 'Stella Blue' (6)
11. Flowering tobacco, *Nicotiana alata* 'Nicki White' (6)

SQUARE CORNER PLANTER

1. Weeping western cedar, *Juniperus scopulorum* 'Tolleson's Green Weeping' (1)
2. Bird's-nest spruce, *Picea ables* 'Nidiformis' (3)
3. Threadleaf coreopsis, *Coreopsis veriscillata* 'Zagreb' (3)
4. Variegated annual vinca, *Vinca major* 'Variegata' (3)
5. French marigold, *Tagetes patula* 'Janie Flame' (7)
6. Common garden petunia, *Petunia × hybrida* 'White Cascade' (2)

WINDOW BOX

1. Geranium, *Pelargonium × hortorum* 'Orbit Scarlet' (3)
2. Common garden petunia, *Petunia × hybrida* 'White Cascade' (4)
3. Browallia, *Browallia speciosa* 'Blue Troll' (5)

FREESTANDING POTS AND PLANTERS

1. Climbing miniature rose, *Rosa* 'Snowfall' (1)
2. Miniature rose, *Rosa* 'Debut' (3)
3. Browallia, *Browallia speciosa* 'Silver Bells' (3)
4. Common garden petunia, *Petunia × hybrida* 'Ultra Crimson Star' (2)
5. Zucchini, *Cucurbita pepo* var. *melopepo* 'Green Magic' (1)
6. Joseph's-coat, *Amaranibus tricolor* 'Illumination' (1)
7. Sour cherry, *Prunus cerasus* 'North Star' (1)
8. Everbearing strawberry, *Fragaria nescia* 'Tristar' (12)
9. Rose geranium, *Pelargonium graveolens* (1)
10. Swiss chard, *Bela vulgaris* 'Burpee's Rhubarb' (3)
11. Garden lettuce, *Lactuca sativa* 'Green Ice' (5)
12. Pak-choi, *Brassica rapa* 'Mei Qing Choi' (5)
13. Cucumber, *Cucumis sativus* 'Park's Burpless Bush' (1)

14. Zinnia, *Zinnia elegans* 'Rose Pinwheel' (6)
15. Snap pea, *Pisum sativum* 'Sugar Snap' (8)
16. Rocket larkspur, *Consolida ambigua* 'Dwarf Blue Butterfly' (3)
17. Shrub rose, *Rosa* 'Bonica' (1)
18. Ageratum, *Ageratum boustonianum* 'Adriatic' (3)
19. Common garden petunia, *Petunia × hybrida* 'Yellow Magic' (3)
20. Sweet alyssum, *Lobularia maritima* 'Carpet of Snow' (3)
21. Common basil, *Ocimum basilicum* 'Spicy Globe' (1)
22. Soapweed, *Yucca glauca* (1)
23. Dill, *Anethum graveolens* 'Bouquet' (1)
24. Fennel, *Foeniculum vulgare* (1)
25. Garlic chive, *Allium tuberosum* (1)

26. Oregano, *Origanum vulgare* (1)
27. Lemon thyme, *Thymus × citriodorus* (1)
28. Summer savory, *Satureja hortensis* (1)
29. Spearmint, *Meniba spicata* (1)
30. Italian parsley, *Petroselinum crispum* (1)
31. Common basil, *Ocimum basilicum* (3)
32. Creeping rosemary, *Rosemarinus officinalis* 'Prostratus' (1)
33. French lavender, *Lavandula deniata* (1)
34. Common sage, *Salvia officinalis* (1)

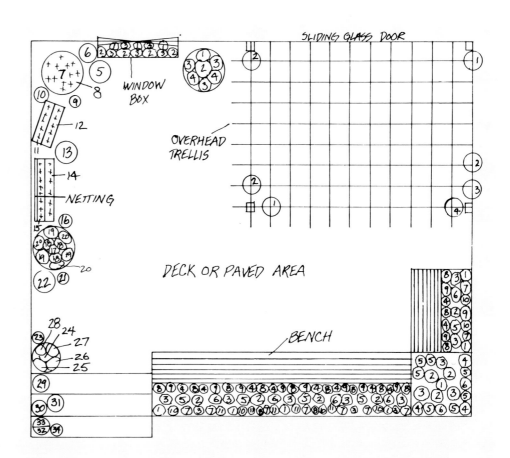

Part Two

ARBORS
AND TRELLISES

WARREN SCHULTZ

INTRODUCTION

There is a basic rule of gardening, an irrefutable law of the landscape that can be called the principle of verticality. Simply put, gardens are visually improved by the addition of vertical elements. And it follows that arbors and trellises are ideal considerations for adding vertical interest, particularly since they lend attractive support to all types of clinging, hanging, and dangling plants.

Arbors and trellises can influence a garden in many ways. They can add a touch of elegance. Sometimes, they create a spot to sit and stretch out with a good book, or they might just offer a good garden vantage spot, out of the glaring sun. They can also provide privacy by screening certain areas from view or by offering a secret place for a rendezvous or just a place to escape.

In addition to creating a mood, arbors and trellises offer a very concrete benefit to the landscape: They increase your gardening space. You can squeeze more plants into the same place if they're growing up, and plants often fare better because they receive more sun. They also benefit from disease-discouraging breezes. Plants take on a whole new dimension when they're allowed to grow up—and the best way to encourage a plant to climb is by introducing an arbor or trellis.

Finally, these structures offer more versatility in the landscape. They can immediately transform a plain, flat lot into something special.

ABOVE: Designed to lift plants closer to the heavens, arbors add a new dimension to the landscape. The roses on this arbor have been raised to a special, lofty position and appear to be clouds floating above the green shrubbery.

OPPOSITE: Arbors can act as doorways in the landscape, marking the passage from one outdoor room to another. Sometimes, they draw you into a deep, dark, and mysterious place; at other times, they form the entranceway to a wide vista beyond the garden. Pass through this arbor and you will enter an enchanted room, where the scent of hanging bougainvillea fills the air, making it a doubly delightful spot to relax and contemplate the garden.

OPPOSITE: An arbor can serve as an attention-grabber to high-light a plant. This deep green arbor and accompanying lattice fence show off the *Clematis montana* 'Rybrum' in its best pink light. It's an inviting feature, beckoning passersby to stroll beneath it.

ABOVE: Trellises and roses go together like love and marriage, with trellises providing the stalwart background support for the ramblings that wander up and down throughout the years. Here, the bright, clean white of the trellis attracts the eye and creates a classic combination with the stunning red roses.

ABOVE: Sometimes a landscape setting calls for a delicate hand. When climbing plants are light and airy and you want to highlight their blossoms without competition, it's best to erect an arbor that is simple in design and material. Honeysuckle takes center stage here, rising above the iris on simple wire arbors. An avid climber, honeysuckle would creep along the ground if it weren't given a structure to climb, until it eventually found a tree to use as support.

OPPOSITE: Trellises don't have to impose to make a statement. Nor do they have to be flat and two-dimensional. With curves and inner space that add depth to a garden planting, this iron cylinder serves as a basket for annual sweet peas.

ABOVE: In some instances, arbors can be created without any construction at all. An intriguing feature for a naturalistic landscape, this allée of mountain laurel has no visible means of support; the plants have been trained to meet in an arch to form a natural arbor.

OPPOSITE: Trellises are essential for some plants. There are many vines that virtually cannot be grown without providing a good measure of support. However, trellises don't always have to be heavy-duty, engineered, permanent structures. These lightweight bamboo trellises are just perfect for temporary plants such as these sweet peas.

ABOVE: Trellises can be used for design as well as function. The ancient art of espalier enables a fruit-loving gardener to train this apple tree against a wall in a design reminiscent of a French *jardin potager*. In addition, espaliering fruit trees greatly increases the amount of fruit that can be harvested from a small area.

LEFT: Arbors and trellises can be relied upon to perform services above and beyond the call of duty. Although this postmodern structure lends an almost expected support for vines, it also functions to provide the landscape with a vertical interest, breaking up the sweeping wildflower meadow.

OPPOSITE: Perhaps best described as an arbor of distinction, a pergola adds an instant air of classical beauty to the landscape, as does the one pictured here festooned with ornamental grape plants. Noted for its sturdy columns and horizontal trellis work, a pergola is best reserved for a large area landscaped in a formal fashion.

ABOVE: When called upon, trellises can also be utilitarian. Here, green metal posts that have been run into the ground in front of an adobe wall disappear into the foliage of 'Blaze' roses, making it appear that the roses are clinging to the smooth wall. Climbing roses, which are actually reluctant climbers at best, will benefit from this encouragement but often need to be tied as well to stay in place.

ABOVE: Arbors often appear as sturdy pillars of strength, anchoring a landscape and making it seem more rooted and permanent. Here, rough, natural wood adds to that feeling of permanence while it also creates a rustic image that instantly ages the landscape. It's a perfect form to complement the wild and far-ranging wisteria.

OPPOSITE: Arbors can be striking even when the plants they feature are dormant. This *Laburnum* tunnel tempts the passerby to stroll through it, even without the flowers in bloom.

THE ARTISTRY OF ARBORS

An arbor usually adds an old-fashioned, leisurely feel to a landscape. It encourages strolling, tempts us to slow down, to stop and smell the roses. Arbors can evoke many other moods, however, and from classical pergolas to stark ultramodern structures, a single arbor can help define the style of the garden. Whether modern, rustic, Victorian, or formal, it's amazing how much impact a single structure can have on a garden.

Arbors come in many varied shapes and designs. Some are abbreviated, simple arches with vines growing over them. Others are more elaborate structures, sometimes with long passageways beneath. An arbor can also be designed to be a focal point or destination, perhaps with a bench at the end of a garden path. In any case, all must be designed so that the spans are sufficiently strong to bear plants that can become quite heavy over time.

RIGHT: Say the word *arbor* and something quite similar to this arch of latticework lost in a cloud of fragrant rose blossoms is very likely to spring to mind. The design and material both carry a touch of England, making this old-fashioned arbor just right for a cottage garden meant to evoke landscapes of the past.

OPPOSITE: An arbor may serve as a garden divider. Here, a delicate iron arch marks the path that separates a kitchen garden from ornamental beds. The airy iron work adds a sophisticated element to the food crops and offers visual support not only for the vines growing on it, but also for the foxgloves and aquilegias growing beside it.

OPPOSITE: Arbors can be constructed and planted so that they are light and airy enough to allow other plants to thrive beneath them. This simple, modern timber arbor provides plenty of support for wisteria vines, and they, in turn, provide adequate sun protection for hosta and other shade-loving plants to flourish below.

ABOVE: An arbor can add order to a busy landscape. Here, a tumbled mass of flowers nearly obscures the stone path, but a simple arch draws the eye through the colorful jungle.

ABOVE: Arbors can work magic in the landscape and heighten an appreciation of plants. Greenery can be given a new dimension, making it diverse and full of character when displayed in different forms and shapes. This rustic arbor raises ivy above the ordinary and contrasts the vines with the formally clipped boxwood hedge.

OPPOSITE: A series of simple arches can create a memorable garden feature. Aligned along a path and covered with vines, these arches form a tunnel that opens to the countryside beyond. In the process, the structure conveys a sense of security.

ABOVE: Arbors are often at their best when the design is kept simple; the structure can then serve as a framework to draw attention to a garden element beyond. Here, this perfectly placed arbor takes the shape of an open doorway leading to the statue centered on the lawn in the distance.

OPPOSITE: Often, a plant determines an arbor's style. A simple, unbranched vine, such as this golden hops, calls for a simple arbor. This structure is actually a series of arches united in the landscape by the vining plants. By the end of the season, the arbor will have disappeared completely beneath the growth of the vines.

ABOVE: With its no-nonsense design and crisp lines, this sturdy, stately, and very utilitarian painted wood arbor brings a New England feeling to the garden, while it appears, at the same time, very modern with its straight lines and edges. With clematis growing up the posts and the cross beams holding baskets of bright impatiens, the arbor's plantings ensure color throughout the entire growing season.

ABOVE: It isn't only what's overhead that makes a successful arbor. Decorative posts can offer an interesting transition from the plants below to the plants above, and latticework is an attractive option. In this case, the brick walkway ties the scene together with a pattern that echoes the latticework of the matching posts and overhead trellis.

RIGHT: Nothing beats an arbor's ability to fully engulf a garden in plants. Here, roses are the *raison d'être* for this arbor, but the simple lines of this structure lend itself to the massed plantings around and over it. Stroll through this arbor, and you're surrounded by a richly layered scent of violas, delphiniums, and more.

OPPOSITE: A classical pergola may be a bit overwhelming in many landscapes, but that's where plants can step in to work their magic and soften a bold and perhaps intimidating structure. Here, *Wisteria sintensis* covers the weathered columns, making the pergola a bit less severe, and with the soft and scented blooms holding sway, the rest of the garden doesn't have to measure up to such a high level of formality.

ABOVE: Arbors may be works of art in their own right. This finely crafted arbor is meant to be enjoyed, not obscured by plants, and the wisteria, with its bright panicles exploding from sparse, twisted stems, shows the arbor off to perfection.

ABOVE: Some arbors are designed to complement their surroundings. Instead of attracting all the attention, they can provide a pleasant place to stop and take in the vista, to look beyond the garden and consider it as part of the greater surrounding landscape. This rose arbor provides a break from the hot California sun and creates an idyllic environment for a peaceful afternoon.

OPPOSITE: The unpainted timbers of this rafterlike roof evoke the feeling of a greenhouse without glass. It's clear that the clematis growing up the arch is the star here; there's no fancy woodwork to compete with it for attention.

THE TRADITION
OF TRELLISES

*T*rellises are hardworking garden features that often pass unnoticed when they are covered in a mass of foliage and flowers. Look underneath, however, and you'll be amazed at the variety and ingenuity that goes into these garden structures. You'll see plenty of white lattice fans, of course, but you'll also discover that just about anything that stands upright can serve as a garden trellis.

Trellises can be simple, slapped-together supports in the vegetable garden, or they can be professionally constructed features in the garden hardscape. Most often made of wood, trellises can also be found in other materials, from iron to plastic. They can even be works of outdoor art.

Most importantly, however, trellises need to be sturdy. Their job is to provide a third dimension in the garden, getting plants up off the ground. These structures, therefore, must be well grounded and rot-resistant. Practical considerations aside, a trellis can be the exclamation point that ends a garden declaration.

RIGHT: Annual flowers such as sweet peas and nasturtiums call for support that's light, flexible, and easy to set up and take down. Nylon or jute netting is the perfect solution, working in concert with the plants. Here, casually draped netting suggests a swaying hammock.

OPPOSITE: Trellises often work in tandem with garden walls. The wall provides the vertical strength; the trellis offers a surface for the plants to cling to. Often, they work together visually as well. This gardener has cleverly painted the trellis and wall in colors that match the flowers in the bed in front of them. In this way, the trellis becomes a unifying element in the garden.

OPPOSITE: Vines and brick make a good combination, but sometimes they need a little help in getting together. This clematis clings to the brick wall with the assistance of nearly invisible wires. Trellises are sometimes at their best when they're not seen at all.

ABOVE: This classical fan design made from time-honored materials is perfect for displaying plants at their best. The shape allows plants plenty of room to spread out and adds a whimsical embellishment to the garden.

LEFT: A trellis doesn't have to be constructed of expensive materials or be an elaborate, custom-made design. Here, a length of wire hardware cloth fastened to an adobe wall makes the perfect support for a *Senecio*. In time, the plant will grow to completely hide the trellis.

BELOW: Wooden lattice is an ideal material for trellises. The clingiest plants can hook right into the patterned notches, whereas others, such as this rhododendron, can grow right up through the spaces.

ABOVE: A rustic twig-and-branch trellis is perhaps the most natural-looking way to train climbing plants. Here, this intricately patterned trellis appears as though it has grown right up out of the garden. A trellis such as this can transform any piece of land into a bit of British estate property.

OPPOSITE: In addition to providing support for vines, this simple, geometrically shaped trellis adds visual interest to a walled city garden. The structure fits unobtrusively into the landscape, while its painted green finish warms up the cold brick wall. From a practical viewpoint, you can't beat wood as a trellis material; its surface is soft enough to allow plants to grab on.

ABOVE: We often think of trellises as old-fashioned, but this modern rendition proves that that's not always the case. The large circular space in the center of this structure provides a huge port-hole for viewing the scene beyond. Climbing vines help to soften some of the edges.

ABOVE: This basic trellis design consisting of sturdy posts and a few crossbars is all that's required to create a splendid espalier of apple trees. Allowing plenty of room for the trees to grow, this structure permits a maximum amount of light to reach all the branches.

LEFT: There's virtually no limit to what you can use as a trellis. Plants are willing growers, ready to take on just about any shape or size of support. Here, posts and chains of the type you might expect to find in a parking lot look right at home in the garden once vines have taken over.

OPPOSITE: What could be simpler than two posts supporting a crosspiece? But add some white paint and plant a climbing rose at the base and you have added an elegant embellishment to the garden.

PLANNING FOR PLANTS

*W*hen all is said and done, an arbor or trellis must still play the supporting role; the real stars are the plants that grace them. Ultimately, the success of the structure depends on how well it showcases the plants. And because different vines and flowers call for different styles and materials, arbors and trellises should be planned to harmonize with plants.

A vining plant's ability to cling varies from plant to plant. Some are reluctant climbers and need to be fastened. Others cling by means of tendrils that sprout from stems, leaves, or flowers. Some have aerial roots or thorns that cling to supports. Still others twine completely around any available structure.

When selecting plants, remember that many vines are woodland plants that evolved to climb trees in the forest. They often like to have their heads in the light, with their feet, or roots, in the shade. Deep mulch, approximating the litter on the forest floor, is also appreciated. In addition, vines and climbers may be annuals or perennials; support for perennial plants must be sturdy, as the plants grow in size and weight year after year.

ABOVE: With clinging tendrils that make it an excellent climber, a passion flower adds an exotic element to the landscape. A tropical plant from Brazil, it blooms in warm climes with large blossoms that put on quite a show.

OPPOSITE: Plants are adept at making transitions. Here, *Clematis montana* bridges the gap between garden bed and building. It happily climbs from brick wall to wood trellis, bringing the two elements of this town house garden together in the process.

ABOVE: Most climbing roses are vigorous growers, with their foliage covering even the tallest trellis in a single season. Their shiny foliage is attractive even when not in bloom, but when their flowers do develop and open, they seem made to be presented as only an arbor or trellis can. Roses, however, are not natural climbers. They produce no tendrils or aerial roots, so they must be tied to their support.

ABOVE: Rich purple wisteria clusters complement natural wood. Here, this rustic trellis resembles the texture of a wisteria trunk itself. The wisteria plant calls to mind the outdoor living spaces of mild climates, but the plant is surprisingly hardy, surviving relatively cold winter weather.

ABOVE: A New Zealand native, red parrot beak is best grown as a tropical plant. It's a shrub that likes to climb, with crimson flowers resembling those of sweet peas.

ABOVE: Like all clematis, the stalks of the anemone clematis' leaves act as tendrils to wrap around a support and hold the plant up. Pictured here sporting creamy white flowers, it's also available with pink or rosy red blooms.

ABOVE: With the help of a supporting trellis, the bright purple blossoms of this *Clematis* × *jackmanii* bring color and softness to what would otherwise be a stark garden wall. Strong climbers, members of the Jackmanii Group can grow to great heights.

ABOVE: When grown as a bush or ground cover, honeysuckle loses its full appeal. Only when it's allowed to climb on a trellis or arbor does the beautiful sweet fragrance gain full exposure to the breeze. Honeysuckle arbors are ideal when placed near outdoor living areas where their scent can be fully appreciated.

ABOVE: A shrubby vine that grows virtually anywhere, honey-suckle is such a hearty plant that it's actually been classified as a weed in some parts of the southern United States. The narrow, bell-shaped flowers may be white, red, pink, or orange, and the vines climb by twining around their support. The plants grow well in full sun but actually seem to prefer a bit of afternoon shade.

OPPOSITE: A climbing rose, such as this 'Adelaide d'Orléans', doesn't have to completely cover an arbor to make a statement. Set against this deep green landscape, the fluffy white blossoms stand out as they climb up this otherwise unadorned arbor.

ABOVE: Morning glories may be the fastest growing and blooming of all vines. The broad, papery thin blossoms come in pure white, red, pink, or blue. The vines will grow in nearly any soil and will eagerly clamber over any support, even a garden sculpture.

OPPOSITE: Roses must be carefully trained and tied to supports as they climb along the side of an arbor, seeking to reach the top. Here, the soft pink 'America' roses bring brightness and cheer to this garden walkway, enticing the visitor to continue along the path and pass beneath the light and airy arbor.

ABOVE: Jasmine is an evocative vine. While in blossom, it brings to mind warm, romantic nights on the veranda. With many admirers, its fragrance is considered one of the most beautiful of all flowers. A tender plant covered with bright waxy foliage, jasmine is an eager climber, readily rooting wherever it finds a hint of soil.

ABOVE: The twining vines of wisteria will gladly take the opportunity to grow upward. They are such natural climbers that in the southern United States they are often allowed to grow into trees. With spectacular blooms in purple, pink, or white, it's not difficult to imagine what they can do when provided with an arbor they can call their own.

OPPOSITE: Nothing beats a climbing rose for pumping out masses of blooms, and nothing is better at showing them off than an arbor. With blooms visible above, below, and through the white slats, walking through this arbor feels like being inside a rosebush.

HARDWORKING
ARBORS AND TRELLISES

Freshly painted, beautifully sited, and covered with blooming flora, arbors and trellises may seem like garden sculpture when actually they are, by their very nature, quite utilitarian. They perform specific functions in the garden, providing a surface for plants to cling to or highlighting plants and allowing them to look their best.

Some structures, however, provide even more specialized services. They can allow for an increased harvest and easier picking of fruit or make for healthier vegetable plants by providing more light and air, which discourages diseases. Arbors and trellises may also be erected with people in mind. They can bring needed shade to a hot, dry landscape, provide a lovely spot to sit and enjoy the surroundings, or create some much-needed privacy in a small yard.

OPPOSITE: There's nothing like an alfresco lunch under an arbor to fully appreciate the outdoors. In the landscape, erecting an arbor for fast-growing vines is often the quickest and easiest way to provide a shady respite from the noonday sun.

ABOVE: Where better to perform a June wedding than under a rose-covered arbor? Some, such as this structure with built-in benches, lend themselves naturally to gatherings and ceremonies, providing the feeling of being outdoors while still enclosing the party for a sense of intimacy.

ABOVE: You could set up housekeeping under this arbor. All the necessary elements for enjoying the outdoors are at hand, including a delightful swing. The table and chairs have surely seen many cozy meals by the fire; they could also be moved out into a sunnier section of the garden depending upon the season.

OPPOSITE: An arbor at the end of a boardwalk provides a perfect place for conversation. This one conveys a tropical and rustic feeling, bringing to mind island castaways. It would be hard to resist stopping here under the shady vines.

OPPOSITE: What was once an open corner of lawn has been transformed into an inviting bower with the installation of an arbor complete with a climbing rose. The structure creates a new dimension in the landscape, adding depth and a different perspective to the garden.

ABOVE: Arbors sometimes serve as physical demarcations, border markers, or landscape signs to facilitate the smooth transition from one part of a garden to another. Here, a rose arbor springs up at the confluence of two paths, uniting the separate quadrants in this lush garden.

ABOVE: Dwarf nectarines naturally take to a trellis. By growing the plants trellised in an informal espalier, the gardener can grow more trees in a given space and the fruit will be easier to pick. Stringing the branches against the trellis also opens up the plant to allow more light and air to penetrate to the center of the tree.

RIGHT: Tepees are ideal trellises for beans. Not only are they self-supporting, they also add an interesting accent to the vegetable garden. The twining vines will naturally climb the poles, and in a short time, these bamboo tepees will be completely covered by lush broad bean leaves.

OPPOSITE: This may be the gardener's equivalent of a reclining easy chair. Complete with an old-fashioned chamomile seat (a soothing scent is released when you sit down), this nook is backed by a trellis supporting vining plants and hanging flowering baskets.

ABOVE: There may not be a lovelier way to produce fruit than on an espaliered tree. Here, a single pear tree has been severely pruned for several years and tied to a simple trellis, forming a living fence. An espalier such as this can become a central feature in an edible landscape.

OPPOSITE: A shade house relies on the growth of several types of plants. Here, grapes grow up and over the walls and peak to provide shade for plants below while still allowing cool breezes to penetrate.

OPPOSITE: With selective pruning and the right support, an apple tree can be shaped into an espalier. With energy and light concentrated on them, these ornamental trees produce an abundance of beautiful blooms and subsequently bear a large crop of delicious fruit.

ABOVE: It doesn't take much to get a creeping vegetable up off the ground, giving it the advantages of better sunlight, less moisture that could rot the fruit, and easier picking. Here, plastic pipes covered in netting do the trick. Later in the season, plastic can be tossed over the frame to protect the plants from frost.

OPPOSITE: Grapes may be the perfect crop for the modern edible landscape. They're well behaved, and with just a little pruning, they'll cling gratefully to a trellis or arbor. There's also something luxurious—and perhaps a little decadent—about picking fat clusters of fruit from overhead as you stroll under an arbor.

ABOVE: The best place to find a hardworking utilitarian trellis is in the vegetable garden, and often the first crop that needs support in the spring is peas. In fact, you can't grow many varieties without some sort of supportive device. Netting strung between poles is often the easiest way.

ABOVE: Vegetable garden structures are often simple and ingenious, made on the spot to suit a particular need. Although they may be light and temporary, they must also be strong enough to hold fast-growing vines, such as this chayote, a tropical vegetable that is also known as mirliton.

OPPOSITE: A favorite vegetable crop, tomatoes reap the benefits of trellis life. More plants can be cultivated in less space with fewer diseases and easier harvesting. Tomato plants can certainly be left to sprawl, but growing them vertically may be a gardener's favorite way.

CLIMBERS FOR ARBORS AND TRELLISES

American bittersweet (*Celastris scandens*)

Boston ivy (*Parthenocissus tricuspidata*)

canary vine (*Tropaeolum peregrinum*)

Chinese wisteria (*Wisteria sinensis*)

clematis (*Clematis* spp.)

climbing hydrangea (*Hydrangea anomala petiolaris*)

climbing roses (*Rosa* spp., including White Lady Banks, Himalayan musk rose, and hybrid multiflora ramblers, as well as climbing rose cultivars)

cup-and-saucer vine (*Cobaea scandens*)

cypress vine (*Ipomoea quamoclit*)

garden nasturtium (*Tropaoleum majus*)

honeysuckle (*Lonicera* spp.)

hyacinth bean (*Dolichos lablab*)

kolomikta actinidia (*Actinidia kolomikta*)

moonflower (*Ipomoea alba*)

morning glory (*Ipomoea tricolor*)

Oriental bittersweet (*Celastrus orbiculatus*)

ornamental grape (*Vitis coignetiae*)

passionflower (*Passiflora incarnata*)

scarlet runner bean (*Paseolus coccineus*)

silver lace vine (*Polygonum aubertii*)

sweet autumn clematis (*Clematis maximowicziana*)

winter jasmine (*Jasminum nudiflorum*)

wisteria (*Wisteria floribunda*)

yellow jessamine (*Gelsemium sempervirens*)

A CLIMBING GARDEN

Plant List

(number of plants needed in parentheses)

1. Climbing hydrangea, *Hydrangea anomala petiolaris* (1)
2. Oriental bittersweet, *Celastrus orbiculatus* (2)
3. Silver lace vine, *Polygonum aubertii* (1)
4. Cypress vine, *Ipomoea quamoclit* (1)
5. Cup-and-saucer vine, *Cobaea scandens* (1)
6. Moonflower, *Ipomoea alba* (1)
7. Garden nasturtium, *Tropaoleum majus* (1)
8. Common morning-glory, *Ipomoea purpurea* 'Heavenly Blue' (1)
9. Clematis, *Clematis* 'Niobe' (1)
10. Clematis, *Clematis × jackmanii* (1)
11. Clematis, *Clematis* 'Nelly Moser' (1)
12. Clematis, *Clematis* 'Mrs. Cholmondeley' (1)
13. Clematis, *Clematis* 'Henryi' (1)
14. Clematis, *Clematis chrysocoma* var. *sericea* (1)
15. Clematis, *Clematis texensis* 'Duchess of Albany' (1)
16. Clematis, *Clematis maximowicziana* (1)
17. Clematis, *Clematis macropetala* (1)
18. Clematis, *Clematis* 'Marie Boissciot' ('Mme. LeCoultre') (1)
19. Late Dutch honeysuckle, *Lonicera periclymenum* 'Serotina Florida' (1)
20. Scarlet trumpet honeysuckle, *Lonicera × brownii* 'Dropmore Scarlet' (1)
21. Everblooming honeysuckle, *Lonicera × heckrottii* (1)
22. Climbing rose, *Rosa* 'Dortmund' (1)
23. Climbing miniature rose, *Rosa* 'Jeanne Lajoie' (1)
24. Climbing miniature rose, *Rosa* 'Snowfall' (1)
25. Climbing rose, *Rosa* 'Don Juan' (1)
26. Canadian hemlock, *Tsuga canadensis* (10)
27. Tomato, *Lycopersicon lycopersicum* 'Sweet 100' (1)
28. Tomato, *Lycopersicon lycopersicum* 'Better Boy' (1)
29. Malabar spinach, *Basella alba* 'Rubra' (5)

30. Lima bean, *Phaseolus lunatus* 'Carolina' (5)
31. Pole bean, *Phaseolus vulgaris* 'Kentucky Wonder' (5)
32. Scarlet runner bean, *Phaseolus coccineus* (5)
33. Yard-long bean, *Vigna unguiculata sesquipedalis* (5)
34. Sugar snap pea, *Pisum sativum* 'Sugar Snap' (1 packet)
35. Cucumber, *Cucumis sativus* 'Sweet Sucess' (1 packet)
36. Cantaloupe, *Cucumis melo* 'Jenny Lind' (1 packet)

37. Mixed ornamental gourds (1 packet)
38. Grape, *Vitis labrusca* 'Concord' (1)
39. Trumpet vine, *Campsis × tagliabuana* 'Mme. Galen' (1)
40. Boston ivy, *Parthenocissus tricuspidata* 'Veitchii Robusta' (1)
41. Wisteria, *Wisteria floribunda* 'Ivory Tower' (1)

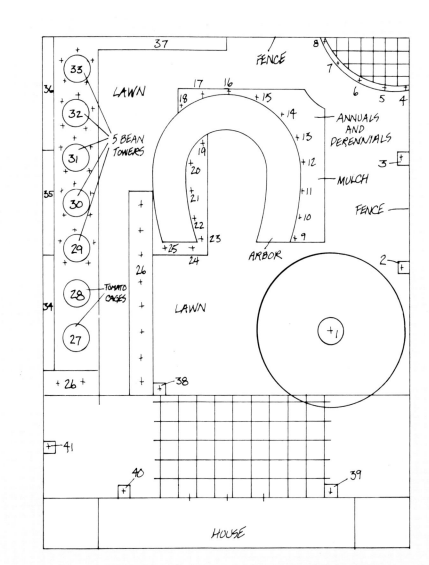

Part Three
SHADE GARDENS

WARREN SCHULTZ

INTRODUCTION

*S*hade. The very word sends chills through most gardeners. To many, shade is synonymous with gloom and bleakness and is often perceived as perilous to garden plants. A lack of sun, however, doesn't have to be a handicap in a garden. In fact, with the wide variety of plants and plethora of designs that are well suited to life in minimal light, it's time to look at shade with a positive attitude.

In the landscape, shade creates a natural time-out. It beckons passersby to stop and rest, making it an ideal spot to place benches and tables. Meandering paths winding through shadows invite a stroll in cool relief from the hot summer sun. Shade also casts an air of mystery as it obscures and blurs and softens hard edges. Certainly, a world without shade would be a desolate and unforgiving place.

Shade is not monolithic, however; it is shrouded in subtleties. Whether it is light, medium, or dark or dappled or fleeting, the wise gardener is glad for a bit of shade and will learn how to use it in the landscape.

ABOVE: A shady spot can become an important feature in the garden, allowing the designer to focus attention on favorite plants. Here, a wise combination of foliage plants offers a variety of cool green colors and different shapes and textures to provide interest throughout three seasons.

OPPOSITE: Wherever you find a stately tree gracing an expansive front yard, you'll find dignified shade as well. Old, tall trees cast a high, dappled shade that's easy to work with. This type of gentle half-shade is ideal for many flowering and foliage plants. Even a finicky lawn thrives under it.

ABOVE: Shade, of course, creates an oasis, a welcome escape from the pounding sun. Out of direct sunlight, this patio is a delightful place to sit and relax and sip iced tea on a hot summer afternoon. The soft white blooms scattered throughout the window boxes and pots accentuate the coolness of the shade.

RIGHT: A shade garden can be wild and naturalistic—as well as brightly colored. With just a little push of the imagination, a woodland setting can be improved with a generous planting of azaleas. Traveling this woodland path evokes the feeling of being submerged in a sea of blooms.

OPPOSITE: A vivid splash of color can add a natural punctuation point to a woodland floor in early spring. With the help of some carefully placed *Narcissus cyclamineus* planted in a casual pattern, this tranquil scene comes alive. Serving to anchor the yellow blooms, a winter currant bush, rarely seen in North American gardens, is dotted with red flowers.

ABOVE: Shade is often the impetus for creating a striking landscape feature. Rather than struggle with growing turf in the shade cast by a wall, this gardener has planted a bountiful bed of impatiens. Abundant with bright blossoms, these mounding plants are perfect for beds, and they'll gladly grow up against buildings where grass won't survive.

ABOVE: Foliage plants rule in the shady border, but just because they lack conspicuous flowers certainly doesn't mean they have to be dull. Here, eye-catching caladiums virtually shout for attention and allow for no mistaking where the path leads.

OPPOSITE: Some trees, such as this old apple, cast only light shade, and their shadows interfere very little with the growing process of the plants around them. In many cases, it's even possible to grow a lawn right up to their trunks.

ABOVE: Shade isn't always an uncontrollable product of nature. Sometimes a small man-made patch of shade can be created for visual interest and to permit the gardener to grow certain plants. This porcelain berry vine shades the window box below, keeping the hot, drying sun from the impatiens.

OPPOSITE: Shade often makes strange bedfellows. The moderate, shifting light of dappled shade allows for combinations not seen in full sun or deep shade. Here, ferns spread in the deepest shade along the trunk of the tree, while primulas and trollius take advantage of the lighter shade along the edge of the bed.

ABOVE: Patio gardens are usually in the shade of a tree or a house, but there are plenty of flowers that sport bright blossoms in less than full sun. Bright begonias are perfect for growing in shaded boxes and pots.

LEFT: Sometimes shade is best left untouched—or seemingly untouched. Visitors strolling down this winding, shady path will be delighted by the single azalea blazing at the bend.

OPPOSITE: Shade can be manufactured or built to suit the gardener. This gazebo provides a shady spot for relaxing among the plants, while also permitting enough light to pass through for plantings to thrive beside it. Even roses bloom vigorously in the dappled light.

GRADES OF SHADE

The face of shade can be as changeable as the weather, and like snowflakes, no two spots of shade are the same. In fact, the degree of shade in a single area of the garden may change from season to season, from day to day, and even from hour to hour. The quality of shade is also determined by what is casting it. A wall or fence will cast a denser shade than a tree or bush. Even the height, type, and age of a tree will make a difference.

However, if forced to squeeze shade into categories, it can be labeled either light, medium, or deep. Light shade is cast by tall trees, medium shade is created by densely branched trees or shrubs, and deep shade is caused by evergreens and buildings. There are plenty of flowers that will welcome a place in light shade, blooming profusely once there. Medium shade often offers enough light for some flowering plants, but this is where foliage plants such as hosta shine. Only the heartiest plants will survive in the deep shade, making it an ideal place for ground covers. If you carefully analyze the shade in your own garden, you should be able to find the perfect plants to suit your shade requirements and your garden design.

RIGHT: Shade comes in all grades and degrees. Many levels are often present in a single garden as such shade-loving plants as azaleas and rhododendrons create an even heavier layer of shade beneath them. In the under-story, interest can be provided by foliage plants. Here, the combination of light and dark shade and undulating levels of glacial outcroppings provide surprises around every turn.

OPPOSITE: High, dappled shade is often the state of affairs in wooded, natural landscapes. The sun isn't completely blocked out but peeks in and out through the trees during the day, so that underplantings such as this foam-flower will receive enough sunlight to thrive.

163

ABOVE: Layers of trees and a substantial brick wall make for different grades of shade. In the fore-ground, where the shade is lighter, a white-flowering shrub provides a bright break. Farther back, tucked into the deep shade of the wall, are foliage plants.

OPPOSITE: Even the most heavily shaded area can have a silver lining. Try breaking up the gloom with selective plantings. Here, a path through a heavily wooded area is accented with tiny wildflowers.

ABOVE: In most yards, there are usually a few spots where the shade is deep enough to create lawn problems. Instead of trying to resuscitate brown turf, take advantage of medium shade by digging out the lawn and replacing it with vibrant flowering beds.

ABOVE: Medium shade, including dappled light from trees, creates a perfect setting for a patio. Offering respite from the sun, the trees shadowing this brick patio let in enough light for flowering potted plants.

ABOVE: Pots brimming with flowers will introduce a jolt of color to a shaded area. Here, begonias are right at home in shallow dishes surrounding the trunk of a tree. Although sunlight falls freely on the garden in the background and the foreground is completely in shade, the sun reaches beneath the tree in early morning and late afternoon, providing enough light for blooming plants. These begonias will bloom happily in the moderate shade provided.

OPPOSITE: Arbors can be used to create light shade and combine two distinctly different types of plants. Here, the sun-loving *Laburnum* thrives as it dangles from the arbor. At the same time, the *Allium giganteum* below receive just enough light shade to keep them fresh and long blooming.

ABOVE: Many gardeners would be amazed at the variety of flowering plants that will bloom quite happily in light shade. In fact, shade can be used to provide relief for sun-loving plants. Here, these apothecary roses won't need as much water during the hot summer months because the ground will stay cooler and moister protected by this canopy of shade at midday.

ABOVE: As shade moves across a garden throughout the day, the dimmer light will cause bright-colored flowers, such as these nasturtiums, to appear deeper in hue. Light shade will also save these blooms from fading too quickly: Note how those flowers on the left already appear to need some relief from the blazing sun.

Making the Most of Shade

*O*nce you've learned to recognize the changing faces of shade, the next step is to figure out how to make the most of it. When planning the garden, think of the benefits of shade and the mood it evokes, and then plan and plant to enhance and work with a shade-filled area, taking advantage of the shade instead of fighting against it.

Offering cool relief, shade provides an ideal environment for a quiet stroll or a peaceful stopping place for relaxation. Paths, for example, are a natural addition to a heavily canopied section of the landscape, while benches and small pools or ponds are the perfect garden embellishments to accent the beckoning and comforting nature of shade. You can incorporate luxurious foliage plants into the setting and interplant them with vibrant annuals that will bloom all summer or perennials that will offer splashes of cheery color. Once you start working with the shade instead of railing against it, you'll be amazed at the options that present themselves.

ABOVE: Ah, the allure of shade. The promise of respite from the sun draws visitors to this rustic wooden bench. The white rhododendrons provide a soothing naturalistic backdrop and encourage a longer stay.

OPPOSITE: A worn stone bench is a natural accoutrement for the deep, deep shade of this setting. Cool and dark like the shade itself, the bench seems almost alive with its color and texture matching the rhododendron and trillium leaves.

ABOVE: Sometimes it is best to give in to shade, taking a cue from its shape and form. Here, a path traces the shade as it winds through the woods. Hosta gracefully edges the woodchip trail, providing a beautiful transition between what is man-made and what is natural.

OPPOSITE: Rather than clearing trees to create an expanse of lawn, this landscape plan took only as much of the woods as needed for an intimate patio. Nestled into a glade of shade, this natural setting has preserved the feeling of living at the edge of a cool woodland. Shade-loving azaleas are appealing in this environment, because even when they are not in bloom, their shiny, waxy foliage is attractive.

ABOVE: No matter where this sun-dappled path leads, its tunnel-like appearance is inviting and irresistible. The light shade cast by the heavily wooded landscape creates an ideal growing environment for this mountain laurel arbor, which wouldn't survive in the direct sun.

OPPOSITE: Shaded passageways and stepping stones seem to be meant for each other. Here, violas grow profusely between field-stones, softening the edges of the walk. It's tempting to stroll bare-foot through this garden, feeling the cool comfort of the stones on your feet.

ABOVE: Medium shade is a classic location for a tranquil garden pool, with many bog and water plants preferring this type of muted light. The water reflects the silhouettes of the overhanging trees, which create a layered, deeper shade.

ABOVE: Living with shade casts it in new light. As you become familiar with your conditions and investigate, study, and monitor your shade, you will discover how you can manipulate the shadows to suit your garden style and design. Here, high-branched trees create shade at midday when the sun is directly overhead but allow in enough light early and late in the day to let a colorful woodland garden flourish. It is also possible to remove some lower tree branches to create sunnier conditions.

RIGHT: A reflecting pool is often the solution to a deep-shade dilemma. It provides visual interest in a spot where perhaps nothing will grow, and the reflection creates the illusion that the area is chock-full of color.

ABOVE: Ground covers make a wonderful lawn substitute in low light conditions. Creating a luscious sea of verdant foliage around a tree, this pachysandra will stay green throughout most of the year and will require virtually no maintenance. A ring of red impatiens cleverly breaks up the color scheme, taking further advantage of the shade.

ABOVE: Pots work wonders in the shade. They can be planted with species such as this *Nicotiana thakham* that will flourish in dim light, or as long as the pots and the plants in them aren't too big, they can be planted with sun-loving species and moved around the garden periodically to capture some rays. In this way, surprising blooms can grace even the darkest spot.

ABOVE: Statuary can be used to brighten a shady spot and add visual interest to predominant foliage. Here, it seems natural to encounter this figure resting for a moment in the shade. It's where we would choose to stop if time permitted.

OPPOSITE: While containers can bring color to dim corners, shade returns the favor. Out of the glare of the sun, plants in pots require less water and care. Here, marguerites and white verbena make fine companions in this urn.

GROUND COVERS AND
FOLIAGE PLANTS

*W*hen standing face-to-face with shade, think green. Foliage plants or ground covers are good choices for the backbone of a shade garden design. The absence of flowers, however, doesn't mean that the beds have to be dull. Ferns, for example, bring the exotic touch of the tropics to a garden, while ivy evokes the ambience of a venerable British estate.

Foliage plants and ground covers combine beautifully with each other and with flowering plants, and there is no shortage of shades, textures, and forms available. Ground covers are certain to grow and spread even in the heaviest of shade; in light shade, they can provide a background or frame for brighter plants.

OPPOSITE: If a large patch of ground cover appears too monotonous, it can be broken up with statuary, hardscape, or landscape features that don't rely on sunshine to bring out its beauty. Here, an elegant statue is spotlighted in a field of pachysandra.

ABOVE: English ivy is the classic, foolproof creeping foliage plant for the shade. There seems to be no nook or cranny too dim for ivy. It creeps, it crawls, it climbs in all but the very darkest of areas. You can cut it, tromp on it, and otherwise mistreat it and ivy will still keep on growing. And through it all, ivy carries a stately, aristocratic air.

ABOVE: Adding a splash of color in medium shade, blue star creeper is a delicate species best used to cover small areas. The small-leaved, low-growing plant is covered with tiny, bright blue flowers from spring into summer.

OPPOSITE: A neatly edged bed of confederate jasmine presents a formal look in this less-than-sunny spot. Easily trimmed with shears or a lawn edger, ground covers can be kept in bounds and shaped to suit any surrounding.

ABOVE: Shady ground covers don't have to be restricted to ground level. Here, *Lamium* creeps along a stone wall, adding a second dimension to the garden and providing unexpected fresh color and texture to an otherwise straightforward retaining wall.

ABOVE: A very vigorous grower, gout weed earns its name. It spreads like wildfire in sunny locations but is much better behaved in shady spots. Here's a good example where shade can be used to control the growth of a plant. This extremely hardy, deciduous perennial is favored mainly for its beautifully variegated cream and green foliage.

ABOVE: Some plants seem to be made for each other as well as for the shade. This artful, fail-safe combination of ferns, hostas, violets, and *Lamium* 'Beacon Silver' includes varying heights, textures, and hues to add depth to a shady spot.

RIGHT: Some gardeners plant trees just for the sake of creating shade to grow hosta. Formerly called funkia and found only in basic green, hosta can be found today in hundreds of varieties that range from green to gold to yellow and come in variegated combinations of them all. Most send up long stalks of small, often fragrant flowers in midsummer.

ABOVE: Hosta are perfect plants to place along a shady walk. Their full, clumplike growth pattern softens the edges of a path and provides lush foliage to tickle the ankles. The plant thrives in medium to heavy shade and loose soil.

ABOVE: Shade is an especially welcome commodity in the heat and humidity found in the southeastern United States. Warm-region gardeners have the option of growing palms and ginger to provide rich, tall foliage as a backdrop to ferns, a favorite where the living is easy.

OPPOSITE: For a touch of the exotic to brighten that patch of sun-deprived landscape, look no further than the ostrich fern. It brings a tropical, junglelike feeling to any garden.

Short-Term Shade Solutions

Shade-Loving Annuals

Gardeners often think of annuals as bright faces for sunny spots, but it's surprising how many annual flowers and vines shine in the shade. Begonias, coleus, and impatiens, among others, will grow fast and take advantage of the changing circumstances throughout the growing season. In addition, annuals are versatile and mobile and can be used to alleviate problem spots in the landscape. They're especially well suited for containers and can provide a vibrant focal point when added to pots, hanging baskets, and window boxes. Many annuals can be started from seed at home. Plan to plant them closely in the shade to take full advantage of their color and form.

RIGHT: Sometimes nothing but color will do—even in the shade. The choices may be limited, but as long as there are impatiens, there can always be color in the garden. In addition to their bright, eye-catching hues, impatiens are also treasured for their growing speed and flexibility. Even under trees or against walls, they grow so fast that they provide almost instant, ground-hiding color.

OPPOSITE: Available in a variety of colors, perky, bushy impatiens grow quickly in the shade to form drifts of everblooming plants. Designs and hues can be changed from year to year or even month to month to provide the best show.

ABOVE: Not a monolithic blanket of dimness, shade is often a very individualized combination of light and dark. The shade on this front porch is dappled with shifting light that's ideal for hanging baskets, window boxes, and pots filled with foliage plants, Boston ivy, and impatiens.

ABOVE: The splashy, variegated leaves of coleus present a colorful twist to this otherwise traditional shade garden. The coleus is a surprising contrast to the classic, bright orange New Guinea impatiens hugging the trunk of the small tree.

ABOVE: Ferns fit nicely into any shady nook. Hardy perennials, they provide a reliable background for annual color. Here, flowering tobacco is tucked in among the fronds, growing amazingly well in light to medium shade and sporting a fine crop of beautiful blossoms. Many cultivars of flowering tobacco are also extremely fragrant, especially in the evening, which will extend the allure of the shady spot into the night.

ABOVE: With huge, rich-colored blooms, tuberous begonias provide incomparable color for shady window boxes, pots, baskets, and beds. If started early in spring, the tubers will quickly grow to provide attractive foliage as well as color throughout the summer.

RIGHT: Shining in this semishady cottage garden, these showy biennial foxgloves will bloom the first season if started early indoors, much like annuals. Although often listed as sun-loving, foxgloves grow well in semishade, their colors even more vibrant out of the bright sun.

ABOVE: Wildflowers can also range into the shade. This packaged mix of thickly sown meadow flowers snuggles up to a tree, creating the illusion of a small meadow bursting with blooms in this flower-filled backyard.

OPPOSITE: The light shade cast by high-branched trees creates some interesting possibilities. Here, shade-loving ivy nestles up against a gleaming ice plant, known primarily as a sun lover. It will bloom profusely, however, in light shade, and although it's a perennial in this California garden, it must be treated as an annual in cooler climates.

PERMANENT SHADE SOLUTIONS
SHADE-LOVING PERENNIALS

Shade grows deeper and expands over the years as shade-casting trees grow taller and more dense, making shade-loving perennials a good garden bet. Set them in the earth and perennials make themselves at home in the shadows, spreading out as the years pass and making the spot their own.

From astilbe to dicentra to viola, there are plenty of perennials that are made for the shade. With a seemingly limitless gallery of colors, forms, and blooming seasons to choose from, perennials are the way to go when you want to give a sense of permanence to your shade bed.

ABOVE: Azaleas make a spectacular statement in the shade. Native woodland plants, they don't pine for sunshine but bloom their best in dappled light. They can be planted closely together to create a hedge of color in early to midspring. The hardy bushes can be left to grow at will or trimmed to control their shape and size.

OPPOSITE: Azaleas can create quite an impact when sprinkled throughout a woodland garden. Planted as specimens, they are a pleasure to stumble upon while strolling along a woodland path. Azaleas are fast and easy growers provided they are planted in slightly acidic soil.

ABOVE: In addition to color, shape and texture create a memorable effect in the shade. Here, the hedge in the foreground has been sculpted to present azaleas at their best. Although the flowering plants represent only a fraction of the plantings here, they present more of an impact because of the artful trimming.

ABOVE: Rhododendrons explode with huge, popcorn-ball blooms early in spring. They seem to shine from within and brighten the shadows around them. Here, in medium shade, the bushy plants pair nicely with the ground-hugging trillium below.

OPPOSITE: A vigorous bloomer in shade throughout the summer, feathery astilbe can be paired with other shady bloomers for maximum effect. Here, planted in combination with astilbe, primulas show off their delicate pastel blooms by shooting them forth like fireworks on slender stems above low, prostrate foliage. The hosta in the right corner provides a broad-leaved exclamation point, and it too will bloom later in the season.

ABOVE: Flaring like tongues of pastel flame, astilbe blossoms bring cheer to the shade. A popular shade-loving herbaceous perennial, this species is well loved for its soft, soothing colors and ferny foliage.

ABOVE: With its intense yellow and orange flowers, the cowslip primrose is a common sight in meadows and along roadsides in Europe. Shown here in a garden in the United States, the plants make wonderful partners for Virginia bluebells. Both are at their floriferous best in spring.

OPPOSITE: The pendulous blooms of bleeding heart dangle abundantly in early spring in all but the darkest shade. When the flowers appear, each shaped like a perfect little heart, it becomes clear where the plant's name came from. The foliage is also attractive, although it usually dies back in the heat of summer. In this garden spot, the vibrant ajuga will hide the scanty bleeding heart foliage throughout the summer.

ABOVE: Shady areas are often moist as well, but fortunately there are several perennials that thrive under these conditions. Here, stately *Ligularia* sends up long stalks of bright yellow blooms in midsummer, making a spectacular statement at the edge of a shady walkway and a delightful companion to Matilija poppies and daylilies.

ABOVE: Columbine adds a dainty touch to the shady bed or border. The nodding tubular blooms appear in clear, bright colors of white, red, violet, orange, pink, and more. There are many hybrid varieties that can be easily grown from seed. Very hardy plants, columbines will bloom freely the year after they are sown.

ABOVE: Daylilies are often found in the brightest of places, but don't get the wrong idea about their sun requirements. Sporting a phenomenal range of colors, most daylilies will gladly bloom unabated throughout the season where there is dappled sunshine or half-shade.

RIGHT: Asiatic natives, lilies will provide a naturalistic or woodland look to the landscape, flourishing in the medium shade of an open wood or wooded environment.

OPPOSITE: A relative of the buttercup, anemones thrive in partial shade. There are many species and cultivars, with showy, five-sepaled flowers in red, white, pink, or purple. Some species spread rapidly and can be naturalized in shady meadows.

ABOVE: European wood anemones bloom in the shade early in the spring. The flowers are small and either white or light purple. They're a pretty alternative to spring bulbs in areas that are too shady for tulips or hyacinths.

OPPOSITE: A European native, cyclamen is beginning to make an appearance in North American shade gardens. Although not reliably hardy, cyclamen does do well in warmer climes, producing slightly fragrant red blooms in spring. The foliage is of interest, too, with white etchings along the edges of each leaf.

PLANTS FOR SHADE GARDENS

astilbe (*Astilbe* spp.) Partial or dappled shade

bee balm (*Monarda didyma*) Partial or dappled shade

begonia (*Begonia* spp.) Partial, dappled, or deep shade

bishop's hat (*Epimedium grandiflorum*) Partial, dappled, or deep shade

browallia (*Browallia americana*) Partial or dappled shade

bugloss (*Brunnera macrophylla*) Partial or dapppled shade

carpet bugle (*Ajuga reptans*) Partial, dappled, or deep shade

coleus (*Coleus* × *hybridus*) Partial, dappled, or deep shade

coral bell (*Heuchera sanguinea*) Partial or dappled shade

day lily (*Hemerocallis* hybrids) Partial or dappled shade

fancy-leaved caladium (*Caladium* × *hortulanum*) Partial, dappled, or deep shade

fern species (including *Adiantum pedatum*, *Dryopteris* spp., *Osmunda* spp., *Polystichum* spp.) Partial, dappled, or deep shade

flossflower (*Ageratum* spp.) Partial or dappled shade

fuchsia (*Fuchsia* × *hybrida*) Partial or dappled shade

hosta or plantain lily (*Hosta* hybrids) Partial, dappled, or deep shade

impatiens (*Impatiens wallerana*) Partial, dappled, or deep shade

Jacob's ladder (*Polemonium caeruleum*) Partial, dappled, or deep shade

lily of the valley (*Convallaria majalis*) Partial, dappled, or deep shade

long-spurred columbine (*Aquilegia* hybrids) Partial shade

pachysandra (*Pachysandra terminalis*) Partial, dappled, or deep shade

periwinkle (*Vinca minor*) Partial, dappled, or deep shade

Siberian iris (*Iris sibirica* hybrids) Partial shade

Solomon's seal (*Polygonatum biflorum*) Partial, dappled, or deep shade

spiderwort (*Tradescantia* × *andersoniana*) Partial or dappled shade

wild bleeding heart (*Dicentra eximia*) Partial, dappled, or deep shade

yellow archangel (*Lamium galeobdolon*) Partial, dappled, or deep shade

A SHADE GARDEN

Plant List
(number of plants needed in parentheses)

1. Fuschia, *Fuschia* × *hybrida* or Skaugum begonia, *Begonia worthiana* in pots on pedestals (3)
2. Fancy-leaved caladium, *Caladium* × *hortulanum* (18)

3. Christmas fern, *Polystichum acrostichoides* (28)
4. Plantain lily, *Hosta* 'Shade Fanfare' (3)
5. Royal fern, *Osmunda regalis* (15)
6. Lady fern, *Athyrium filix-femina* (6)
7. Cinnamon fern, *Osmunda cinnamomea* (6)
8. Ostrich fern, *Matteuccia struthiopteris* (12)
9. Plantain lily, *Hosta* 'Frances Williams' (3)

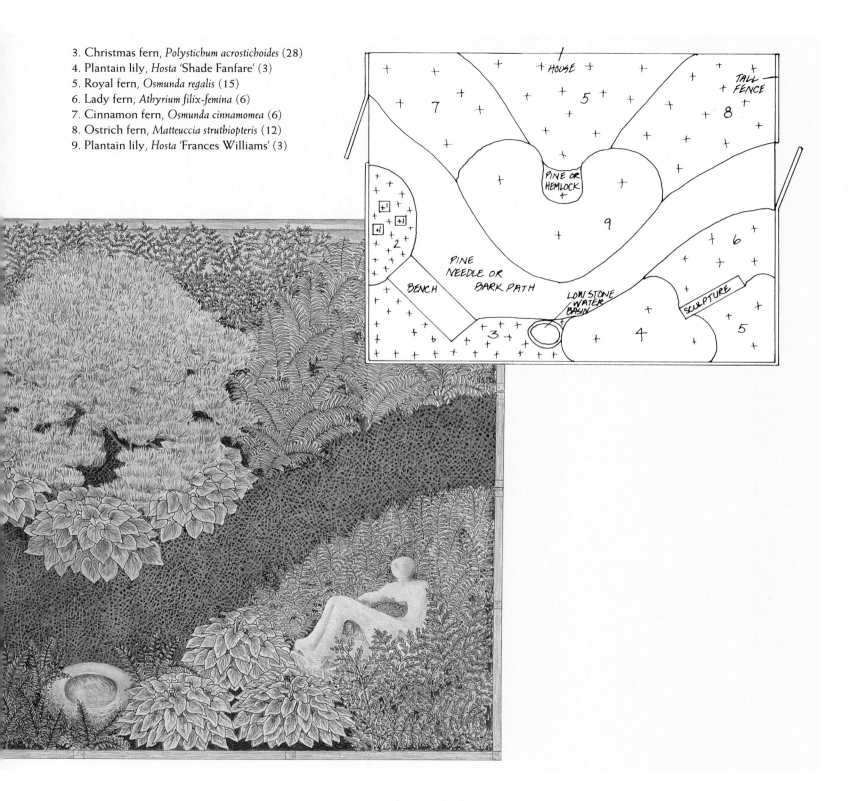

Part Four
WATER GARDENS

CAROL SPIER

INTRODUCTION

*T*o think of a water garden is to envision a glassy pond padded with flat green lily leaves and roseate blooms, sharp iris blades piercing here and there through the sun-dappled surface, and perhaps, the bright flash of a goldfish darting in and out of duckweed shadows or a moss-covered fountain rippling the surface with graceful arcs of water. Water gardens seem inevitably to whisper of magic, hint at mystery, and tease the senses with delight—perhaps because the water, which is so crucial to all plant and animal life, takes on a life of its own, catching the light of the sun and moon, stirring under the wind or rain, and reflecting and echoing the foliage, architecture, and clouds that frame it.

Water gardens can be designed in any size or shape, and any landscape plan can be enhanced by one. Water gardens (or planted pools or ponds—the terms are interchangeable but all refer to bodies of water in which some form of vegetation is growing) can be small or large, sunken permanently in the ground or set above it in a tublike container. They can be regular and geometric in shape or free-form and organic. They can have clean edges and an orderly arrangement of plants, which will give them a formal appearance, or they may be casually arranged, perhaps edged with rocks softened by cascading vegetation and planted in an apparently haphazard manner, which will give them a naturalistic or infor-

mal appearance. They can play a dominant role in the landscape's design, assuming a central or focal position, or they can be placed discreetly, providing an element of surprise each time they are discovered.

INTEGRATING A WATER GARDEN WITH YOUR LANDSCAPE

The particulars of water garden design will be dictated by individual circumstances—the size of your yard, the climate in which you live, and the amount of time and money you wish to invest—but you can design a garden that is as sedate or exuberant as you desire. Devote some thought to the architectural style of your home and to any landscaping that already exists so that your garden can be integrated successfully, decide whether you want a prominent or secluded pool, and then give your imagination, whim, and fancy free reign.

ABOVE LEFT: This long, narrow lily pond set in a hedge-enclosed garden is formal but mysterious. The rows of plane trees create a secluded environment that is enhanced by the secret chamber tucked in under the double stairway. An ivy-covered mount such as this may be absolutely artificial but lends a wonderful feeling of antiquity to the setting and provides a lovely vantage point for contemplation, as do the benches at the edge of the green.

OPPOSITE: A groomed and manicured parklike setting is the classic environment for a large formal water garden. This one has a modified cruciform and is sparsely planted; the regular, controlled arrangement of shrubbery and flower pots is mirrored on the clean expanse of water. The overall landscape is flat and rectilinear within an evergreen frame; low-clipped boxwood parterres outline beds planted with blocks of blooming seasonal color and lead onto an expanse of lawn. The flat stone pond surround is a frame within a frame; the water garden itself provides an elegant focal point that is punctuated by the upright clumps of irises and the silver mounds at each corner.

RIGHT: Water gardens need not be part of a formal vista. Here, an irregularly curved pond spills out of an herbal border just a few steps from the house. Carved into the bank of a stream that meanders across the property, this pond is edged with flat native stone and planted with a few lilies. The effect is gentle and subdued: the cool green and silver vegetation contrasts with the warm brick and stone, the assorted textures complement the rustic setting, and the smooth water trails informally into the passing stream.

LEFT: This paisleylike pond breaks up a long, narrow yard, which is walled in by evergreens that at first glance give the garden a formal appearance. In fact, the plantings curve, spill, and meander through the space with contrived naturalism. The curves make the space less narrow and lead the eye pleasantly through the three distinct sections of the landscape.

OPPOSITE: The irregular stones that form the bank of this rectilinear water garden are softened with tufts of greenery and bordered by pebbled paths, giving it the appearance of a natural stream. The large terra-cotta urns that dot the verges make a nod toward formality, but the confines of the garden, the rocky edging, and the sprays of daylilies have an aura of disorder that is charming and casual.

OPPOSITE: This beautiful round lily pond is set between a rolling lawn and a lovely perennial border. The sharp grassy edge and elegant bench lend the setting formality while the rocky shore and lush foliage provide a naturalistic balance; this yard is large enough for such a transition to be made without effort. The small statue appears to be contemplating the charm of her reflection in the pond.

TOP RIGHT: In a confined garden, a tiny planted pond can elicit a smile of pleasure each time it is discovered. This small walled garden is really no more than a narrow pathway along the side of the house, but it has been carefully planted with well-proportioned shrubs, perennials, and annuals. The curving pattern of the brickwork widens the space and invites the eye to search for details. The water garden is an organically shaped pond with one boggy edge that allows a variety of moisture-loving plants to thrive—and mask the water with a bit of green secrecy. If you live in an urban or town house environment where yards are small, you might contemplate a garden such as this.

BOTTOM RIGHT: A small water garden can provide a focal point in a small garden as effectively as in a large parklike one. This walled garden is very serene; the woven brick pattern and concentric right angles are formal but not austere. The importance of the pond in the center of this primarily shady space is emphasized as it catches the passing rays of the sun and moon. In a small space such as this, simple plantings in a limited palette enhance the quiet, serene mood, as do the terra-cotta animals that pose with everlasting and whimsical concentration.

ABOVE: A raised water garden brings its charms closer to hand, particularly if it is built with broad walls that beckon the visitor to come and sit alongside. In this case, a multilevel raised pool forms part of a border that surrounds a small lawn. The gardens here are fabulous, lush, and colorful, and although the pool is massive, its proportions are balanced by the tall ornamental grass, the exuberant roses, and the broad floral borders. The stone terrace, veined with creeping greens, helps to ease the transition from water garden to floral borders, and bits of stone wall add needed weight to the opposite edge of the lawn.

LEFT: There is no reason not to tuck a tiny water garden into a deep floral border. Here, one is half-hidden by greens and blooms, which comes as a lovely surprise when discovered while strolling along the garden path. The rocks that surround this pool have a marvelously textured surface that is complemented by the dappled water and dense lily pads, and the pool, tucked amid lavishly planted stock, poppies, delphiniums, ivy, and ferns, is intimate.

ABOVE: A round formal garden very often features radiating pathways framing beds of massed plantings. On this brick terrace, a lily pond takes the place of a central flower bed, contrasting but balancing the blocks of red and white impatiens. The effect is orderly and controlled, but the formal design is softened by the mossy surface of the bricks and the lavender that is growing at the water's edge.

OPPOSITE: The use of small geometric beds set into a frame need not be limited to formal gardens. This charming garden features regularly shaped beds dropped somewhat casually into a lawn. The water garden in the foreground, with its sloping brick border and cascading urns, is as well-worn as the the other beds, but in this garden, there is order within what first appears as disorder, and the overall effect is harmonious.

WATER GARDEN EDGINGS

Unless you happen to have a natural pond in your yard, the edging of your water garden will in all likelihood have to be set in place by you, but the material you use and the way in which you assemble it will give your garden a man-made or a natural-looking edge. Man-made edgings include those of preformed tubs or site-poured pools, which might be fiberglass or concrete or even the edge of a sunken wooden barrel, and also those that are permanently assembled of materials such as cut stone, concrete slabs, wood, or ceramic tile. Naturalistic edgings look as though they grew in place and may be created with landscaped vegetation, piled or scattered rocks, sand, mulch, pebbles, or a combination of these.

Man-made edgings are often, but not always, formal in appearance, while naturalistic edgings tend to be, but are not always, informal. A water garden's edging has as much or more effect upon the overall style of the garden as the plantings within it; it will be apparent through all seasons and should be compatible with the shape of the pond and complement your landscape design.

MAN-MADE EDGINGS

While all man-made pond edgings are hard to the touch, they may be smooth or highly textured, matte or shiny, and colored to blend or contrast with the water and foliage. Select your materials for the contribution they will make to the design of your garden, and consider whether they will enhance or compete with the vegetation or other elements of the setting.

ABOVE: Stone-edged and rectangular, this pond seems less austere than the one on the opposite page because it is tucked more intimately into its setting. Spiky daylily leaves spill over the stones to meld with massed waterlilies; taller spiky clumps of yucca rise at the end, their height echoed by a lovely wrought-iron gate that indicates that this is a private or secret place.

OPPOSITE: Here, stone slabs set in mortar border a formal pool. The clean edge of the stone cuts crisply against the grass and the glassy surface of the water and harmonizes with the lovely pergola at the far end. A great clump of yellow flag iris punctuates each corner of the pond and lilies float in graceful swathes across it. The design of this garden could not be more simple, but the space it occupies is grand; it is both serene and imposing.

ABOVE: An artfully constructed stone wall gives this water garden an informal, naturalistic appearance that belies the effort made to create it. The densely padded surface of the water, the irregularities of the stone wall, and the soft cascading greenery shot with colorful blooms are all textural elements that draw the eye in admiration.

ABOVE: Beautifully painted glazed ceramic tiles give this pool a formal look, but the setting, tucked amid dense shrubbery, is mysterious rather than mannered. The pool is lined with deep blue tiles, which intensify the reflected sky and foliage, and the anomalous rock formation and hunk of glass heighten the esoteric atmosphere. Tiles such as these command a lot of attention and may compete with or be lost in their surroundings; this pond is very simply planted so as to balance the busy setting.

ABOVE: A simple plank deck sits right over the edge of the soft liner of this informal water garden in the southwestern United States. The climate in this area is warm and dry, and the deck provides an easy, low-maintenance way to enjoy both sun and pond.

LANDSCAPED EDGINGS

As you select materials to use in a landscaped pond edging, consider the contrasts of height, color, and texture that are available in the hard elements you might use, such as rocks or sand, and in the vegetation that might grow at the shore. Visit your local nursery to find out what types of moisture-loving plants will thrive in your climate, and remember that while there are many plants that can grow in standing water, there are others that love the shallow, damp soil that might ring a pond or that can be planted in the crevices of a rock wall or terrace.

ABOVE: The pool in this formal garden is an extension of the elegant green in which it sits. The parklike space is broken only by the straight lines and planes of hedges and terraces; the beautifully groomed lawn rolls serenely to the water's edge, where the glint of sunlight and the texture of the lilies gently articulate the transition from lawn to pool. The edging of this pool, while made of grass, is one of several carefully contrived elements in the setting, and the effect is far from naturalistic.

235

ABOVE: Here is a water garden that looks as though it occurred naturally. Its edges are a bit ragged and punctuated by sprightly grasses and cattails; greenery seems to spill from water to shore and back again. This small pond sits between a lawn and a perennial border, where it offers a delightfully untidy surprise each time it is discovered.

OPPOSITE: This large woodland water garden could also be the work of Nature herself. The woods slope gently down to the far edge of the pond, where the shore is dotted with rocks. Moisture-loving forget-me-nots spread in carefree abandon over the mulched path along the left bank, which leads past an azalea before wandering into the wood. The pond itself blends into the shoreline with stands of irises and ornamental grasses.

RIGHT: Ponds edged with vegetation need not feel quite so abandoned as the one on the previous page. Here, irises, lilies, and moisture-loving grasses ring a small pond, but they in turn are bordered with irregular paving stones; the effect is naturalistic but contained.

LEFT: With marvelous stone terraced steps leading down to the lily pond, this setting relies on harmonious variations of color and texture for its charm; the terrace is veined with creeping herbs, a bank of mounding artemesia echoes the stony pattern, and small stone pools and beds of greenery meld the lily-dotted water with its surrounds.

OPPOSITE: Though tiny, this deep-set pond is arresting. Bordered with organically shaped rocks that are a bit out of scale for its size, the pond catches and draws the eye. The odd shape, rough rocks, pendulous evergreens, surprise of the spiking iris leaves, and darting of the fish all emphasize an intriguing lack of symmetry.

RAISED WATER GARDENS

When a water garden is raised above ground level, it adds architectural as well as horticultural interest to your landscape. And of course, the closer the surface of the water is to the viewer's eye, the easier it is to admire. If the walls of a raised garden are broad enough, they can double as a delightful bench. The basins or pools that form raised water gardens are almost always preformed or sturdily constructed on site, so they tend to have a formal, rather than naturalistic, appearance. However, the style of the container, the way it is planted, and the setting in which it is placed can soften the look.

Raised water gardens are often quite small. They can be planted in purchased containers and set on a terrace or deck or partially submerged at a focal or hidden place in the yard. Larger raised water gardens are frequently placed at the center of a clearing or a formal garden, or integrated with a paved terrace.

ABOVE: A lily pond at the center of this intimate clearing is an excuse to indulge in quiet contemplation. The slightly raised pond is smooth, round, and serene; it is the perfect enhancement for a classic setting like this, where the stone bench, blooming santolina, and graveled path contribute to the cloistered mood.

OPPOSITE: This oval water garden links the terrace of an elegant waterside home with a small lawn and complements the natural expanse of water below. Although imposing by virtue of its size and setting, it is very simply planted with containers of ornamental grass and appears contemporary and unfussy.

ABOVE: This pitted stone urn has perhaps graced the center of this perfectly paved terrace for most of remembered time. When the seasons smile upon them, the lilies and grass within it make a small show of splendor; otherwise they fade into antiquity with their environment.

RIGHT: It can be difficult to successfully integrate diverse elements in a small space, but here, squares and rectangles and wood, brick, and stone have been carefully arranged to create an inviting walled retreat. With no real room for a bench in this garden, the raised pond offers a surprising and pleasant place to rest. The little geyser fountain lightens the pond and echoes the wonderful tall stalks of digitalis and the posts of the lattice; the eye moves up and around to enjoy the space.

ABOVE: Placed in the middle of a sunny terrace, the pentagonal walls of this water garden make an unusual and rather formal frame for the casual planting within. Bright white in the sunlight, the stone slabs stand in stark but not displeasing contrast to the water, rock, and greenery.

ABOVE: Fieldstones embedded in concrete give this raised pond a rugged, rustic look that would complement a Craftsman-style house—or any vernacular stone dwelling. Although the slender lines of the formal white bench seem oddly juxtaposed with such a heavy pond, the gardens are robust and provide a good balance.

ABOVE: A show-off container such as this bronze basin will look most effective if it is planted quietly. White blooms set against green leaves are an elegant choice to crown the patina-masked relief of the basin, particularly when placed, as it is here, within formal white walls.

RIGHT: Raised water gardens—like sunken ones—can be tucked into beds and borders for an element of surprise or mystery. Even in a very small space, such as the corner of this walled garden, a little planted pond can be a great discovery. Nestled beneath small rhododendrons, this one—complete with goldfish and duck-weed—is a common half-barrel of the type available at any nursery. As in some Japanese gardens, the ground has been covered with pebbles, which provide a lovely setting for the variegated foliage above.

ABOVE: If a raised water garden is small enough, it can be placed among other potted plants. This one, in a green basin, has been topped with a sheet of glass (note the spacers that allow air to reach the garden) to make a witty outdoor end table for a patio.

OPPOSITE: When a raised water garden is set amid lively vegetation, it begins to look as naturalistic as a sunken pond with overgrown edges. Here, an exuberant flower bed embraces a rather small pond, the quiet water set off by a profusion of purple and the happy birdhouse that stands guard.

MOVING WATER

*W*hile still water provides a glassy surface that turns a water garden into a reflecting pool with a serene or austere character, moving water adds a touch of grace, frivolity, or sensuality. Just as ocean waves or river currents mesmerize the passerby, a fountain spray that arcs in rainbow droplets or an ever-changing waterfall cause one to pause and pass into reverie. Moving water, whether quietly flowing or playfully dancing, is somehow irresistible.

Water can flow through a planted pool in the manner of a stream, perhaps cascading over several terraced levels, or it can spout, spray, bubble, or trickle above it through a fountain. Unless you are planting an existing streambed or natural spring, you will need to install an electric pump for circulation. A fountain itself can be sculptural, elaborate and showy, or simple and unobtrusive; a waterfall or cascade can course over rocks or steps, puddling in basins as it moves, or slide down the surface of a retaining wall. Fountains, particularly sculptural ones or those that spray above the water's surface, usually bring a note of formality; cascades and falls may or may not be formal, depending upon the situation. Various styles of fountains are associated with different periods of garden history and with European, Middle Eastern, and Oriental garden styles; when selecting a fountain, you may find it interesting to do some research. A fountain should complement the ambience of its setting; one that is pretentious or incongruous will cheapen rather than enhance the design.

FOUNTAINS

OPPOSITE: The pergola behind this lily pool forms one end of the walled flower garden at Old Westbury Gardens on Long Island. Plumes of water spray in arcs that echo those of the framework beyond; the fountain—a child holding an urn above its head—is diminutive and in proportion with the lilies.

ABOVE: Although the gloriously glazed blue basin that bubbles in the center of this small pool is rather large, its simple shape and gently flowing water settle it into the round frame of the surrounding garden. This setting is particularly beautiful with spring in full, glorious bloom.

ABOVE: A fountain placed to one side of a water garden will have the effect of perpetually filling the pool. If the fountain is sculptural, this narrative quality will be enhanced; here, a satyr, standing appropriately upon a small mound of ivy, pipes water into a quiet garden through his double flute.

OPPOSITE: In an informal water garden, simple jets of water rising magically above the pond's surface may be all that is needed in the way of a fountain. By selecting a fountain that sprays from an invisible source, the design stays simple and uncluttered; here, the shape of the spray repeats that of the foliage.

ABOVE: There is nothing to prevent you from installing a decorative fountain in the tiniest of water gardens; just be sure that it is in proportion to the space. This small pond sits at the base of an old brick wall, which provides the perfect mount for a spouting lion's head. The choice of colors and materials is harmonious so the fountain comes as a pleasant but appropriate surprise.

LEFT: Usually set off by the spare formality of Japanese gardens, a trickling fountain seems equally at home in this naturalistic lily pool settled into the lush background of New Zealand foliage. The simple horizontal pipe is cast to replicate bamboo, and water flows through it into a spherical stone basin, which fills and glistens continuously from the overflow. Here, the fountain is eased into its setting by the large spherical finial topping the stone post and echoed in subtle reflection in the pool.

ABOVE: If your water garden is designed with a sense of mystery, perhaps hidden in a shady, over-grown corner, you might want it to summon passersby with the sound, but not the sight, of moving water. A submerged fountain that bubbles just below the surface would be quietly intriguing; you might build a very simple one that springs up from underwater rocks or choose one that tells an eerie tale.

FALLING WATER

ABOVE: The synthetic antiquity of this decaying wall gives focus and importance to a small pool of irises. Piped water overflows from each perfectly tilted terra-cotta vessel to stream slowly into the pool below. The design, while completely contrived and certainly not appropriate to every landscape, is a marvelous juxtaposition of naturalistic elements in a structured setting.

OVERLEAF: Water spills down this magnificent procession of round cast-iron basins into a series of round stone-rimmed pools, making its entry like royalty proceeding down a grand stairway. A garden such as this certainly owes much of its impact to its impressive proportions, but the design is particularly effective because it relies upon the repetition of just a few well-chosen elements.

257

ABOVE: If you so desire, Nature's hand can be supplemented by your own to tame a wilderness proper-ty. The bed of this naturally falling stream has been helped to step down into a pool, and over time, the rocks and pools have grown into the setting, so that there is a feeling of pleasure, but not surprise, when one happens upon the stream.

OPPOSITE: The watery steps that lead to this lily pond take advantage of a natural slope in the land-scape. This is an intimate cascade, its rocky steps softened with water-loving plants and its banks filled with shrubs and perennials; while the scene is charmingly natural, the reality was lovingly contrived.

WATER GARDENS IN BLOOM

*I*f you are planning a water garden, you must of course think not only of the size and shape of the pool and the way it is constructed but also of the plants that will fill it. Indeed, your love of water lilies or Japanese irises might inspire you to create a water garden before you even think of the particulars of the pool itself. The specific plants you are able to grow in your pond and at its edges will be dictated in part by the climate and location in which you live, but there are many species that can be considered—and loved—for the color, shape, texture, and attitude they contribute.

Because most plants have a limited season of glory, it is a good idea to conceive the basic style and construction of your pond so that it will be attractive no matter what the time of year and then select appropriate plants as you would for any other part of your garden, choosing them to carry out a theme, provide continuous bloom, create a particular palette, or thrive with minimum care, as desired. If your water garden is part of a larger garden, make sure its design relates to its environment—the surrounding plants can set off or extend its beauty.

RIGHT: The plantings in this garden are massed so that each makes a strong statement of shape and color. The water lilies will not bloom until later in the season, but their leaves carpet the surface of the pond with green, the purple blooms of the irises punctuate their spiky foliage, and a great drift of red euphorbia leads the eye to the mounds of greenery beyond.

OPPOSITE: Early summer, with its profusion of blooms, is a lovely time for any garden. For the water gardener, it is the season of the Japanese iris. In this garden, there is a wonderful juxtaposition of elegant and robust blooms with exotic foliage.

OVERLEAF: Perennial candelabra-type primroses thrive in moist soil and light shade. Their bright springtime blooms are festive yet delicate at the edge of a naturalistic pond.

263

ABOVE: These two views of a Shropshire garden in summer reveal a pretty pond bordered by showy perennials. A variety of shapes and textures assures that when the blooms have faded the border will retain its interest.

OPPOSITE: Lovely daylilies, which grow wild along so many rural roadsides, lend an old-fashioned, country-fresh feeling to the edge of a water garden. Here, they make an informal transition from rolling lawn to stony shore. There are hundreds of varieties of daylilies; they come in myriad colors and sizes and are easy to establish, spreading quickly to make beds of dancing blooms.

ABOVE: It is not only the glassy surface of water that fascinates. In this small shallow pool, the water is completely obscured by tightly textured foliage that forms an intriguing monochromatic carpet. Punctuated with unusual rocks and tightly contained within its frame, the pond assumes the importance of a piece of sculpture.

LEFT: Textural interest can also be created in a small water garden when you fill it with remarkably disparate plants. Each specimen planted in this tiny barrel is a different shape, size, and texture; the effect is lively and charming.

OPPOSITE: Massed plantings of a single species, intense with repeated shape and color, are often more impressive than random plantings of several interspersed varieties. Here, a band of pickerel weed, with its bright blue flower spikes and heart-shaped leaves dancing in the sun, cuts without affectation across one end of a casual water garden.

ABOVE: Simple symmetrical plantings, which emphasize the regularity of a pond's outline, are an enhancement to a formal water garden, particularly if it is set imposingly within an open lawn or courtyard. Lilies planted in submerged tubs float in controlled rounds of color in each branch of this pool; the formality is continued by the even placement of the urns on the terrace.

RIGHT: Technically speaking, a water garden is a pond in which submerged or floating plants are growing, but if you are not prepared to establish the real thing, you can easily grow a cheater's version without sacrificing any charm. Here, a wire basket is filled to overflowing with summery annuals and then perched atop a pile of stones, where it sits as a cheery filip to a natural stream.

OPPOSITE: When a very small water garden is incorporated into a larger garden, as this one is into a flower border, it should be viewed as just one design element among several. This garden, which is planted with charming old-fashioned flowers, is unified with a few rustic props—the trellis, the tree stump, and the rock ledge around the little pond.

ABOVE LEFT: Naturalistic lily ponds with heavily landscaped verges provide a wonderful opportunity for textural garden composition. Here, massed floating lily leaves carpet the surface but allow glinting light to bounce between them; the foliage along the shore is variously and delicately cut, contrasting gently with the full roundness of the lily pads below.

ABOVE RIGHT: An intense band of pink begonias strengthens the outline of a formal pool. Here, urns of nasturtiums and petunias unite and extend the bright colors of pond and border.

OPPOSITE: Even though the foliage spills into this pond in a continuous green flow, there is a marked textural contrast between the lily pads and landscaping in this subtropical climate. The deeply cut, arching fronds of ferns and palms, dotted brightly with daylilies and fuchsia, extend an exotic, exuberant embrace like a great ruffled collar around the smooth swathe of lilies.

SPECIAL TOUCHES

*A*ll but the most utilitarian gardening is a form of decorating and therefore owes its ultimate aesthetic success to the designer's finishing touches. Certainly a garden may be unaccessorized and still be beautifully complete, but objects made by human—rather than Nature's—hands can add charm, create mood or narrative interest, or importantly, provide structural support or access. Finishing touches for a water garden might take the form of statuary or small sculpture, a bridge to cross the pool, or even stepping stones to place one amid the lilies.

STATUARY

Water garden statuary often represents figures from antiquity that are associated with water or water-dwelling creatures. It can be life-size, smaller or larger, prominently displayed or hidden among the foliage. Stone, ceramic, and metal pieces that are not sealed or glazed will weather over time and grow a patina that will blend with their surroundings, heightening the sense of mystery that so often pervades a water garden.

ABOVE: Here, a water garden is set into a niche in a garden wall, making a damp and shady grotto. A triton (merman) fills the space and points the way to other wonders through a stand of ferns. A niche such as this would command attention even without the statue, but it begs to frame a composition of some importance.

OPPOSITE: A single statue placed at the center of a formal pool draws the eye and initiates a drama for its setting. The maid in the center of the pond is perhaps a naiad, a fresh-water nymph, caught forever gazing into the depths of the pool before stooping to fill the vessels in her arms.

ABOVE: Realistically proportioned animal sculptures can catch the casual observer off-guard with their unnatural stillness. Two doves have stopped for a meal in the middle of this raised garden and a turtle stands with typical torpor where the water breaks over the wall.

LEFT: It takes a good eye to judge proportion when you are placing statuary, but you may find that realism can successfully give way to whimsy. This fish is of course much too large to inhabit the tiny pool from which he springs, and though the frog who watches from among the petunias seems quite shocked to see him, he brings a smile to the human observer, as does the diminutive, verdigris rabbit poised atop a spray of leaves.

ABOVE: The heron is an elegant water bird known for its stealthy walk and patient stance when searching for food. Herons are classic garden ornaments and are readily available from garden furnishings catalogs. This specimen stands quite realistically at the edge of a naturalistic pond.

ABOVE: Sculptural ornaments need not be representational. You might choose a piece that is abstract or use an organic object such as driftwood. You might also select a functional object with pleasing proportions. The water garden set against this low wall is edged with assorted stones. The large stone at the back is a hand-hollowed slab, and the stone basin that sits on it has a simple, pleasing shape. The composition is spare and soothing yet has a quiet intensity as the repeated rounds and hollows draw and hold the eye.

ABOVE: The serenity of this circular pool is enhanced by the muted natural tones of the statue that stands at its center. The juxtaposition of the vividly colored flowers surrounding this calm body of water creates a lovely counterpoint.

LEFT: The placement of this statue by the edge of a free-form pond emphasizes the intimacy of this water garden setting. Here, a long-haired maid relaxes in privacy, leisurely wringing her hair as if she had just emerged from the water.

BRIDGES AND STEPPING STONES

Bridges and stepping stones are functional embellishments that make a water garden easier to enjoy. If your water garden is shaped in such a way that it invites you to explore the opposite shore or walk among the plantings, a bridge or a path of stones will bring you closer to its beauty. Stepping stones can be formally arranged, but they are most often used in naturalistic settings. Bridges can be architecturally impressive or intensely colored, standing in contrast to the plantings, or simple and unobtrusive, blending with the environment. As is true of fountains, there are particular types of bridges that are associated with certain styles and periods of garden design, and you might find it rewarding to study them in some detail before going to the trouble of building one.

ABOVE: Camelback bridges are characteristic features of Oriental gardens, where they not only link one area with another but also provide strategic vantage points for admiring the space and proportions of the garden. The bright red color is typical of bridges built in the Heian period (710–1150) in Japan; this one is quite large.

OPPOSITE: Nature no doubt intended that streams should be crossed; if you are lucky enough to have one as pleasant as this meandering through your yard, you will of course want to reach the other side with ease. The banks of this stream have the look of a cottage garden; the bridge that links them is an unpretentious plank arc that will be softened as it weathers with the passage of time.

ABOVE: Giverny, the home of Claude Monet, has one of the best loved and most famous of domestic water gardens. Monet was very much influenced by what he knew of Japanese gardens when he designed his water garden, and it has a marvelous blend of Oriental and French features. The gently arced bridge at the far end is covered with a wisteria arbor.

OPPOSITE: Zigzag bridges are typical of Oriental gardens, where they are placed just above the water to bring the visitor as close as possible to important plantings. This one is an inviting path amid spectacular Japanese irises.

Plants for Water Gardens

Water Plants

anacharis (*Elodea canadensis* var. *gigantea*)

awl-leaf arrowhead (*Sagittaria subulata*)

blue flag iris (*Iris versicolor*)

bog bean (*Menyanthes trifoliata*)

cattail (*Typha latifolia*)

common horsetail (*Equisetum hyemale*)

fanwort (*Cabomba caroliniana*)

lizard's tail or swamp lily (*Saururus cernuus*)

milfoil (*Myriophyllum aquaticum*)

pickerel rush (*Pontederia cordata*)

Siberian iris (*Iris sibirica*)

water celery (*Vallisneria americana*)

water lily (*Nymphaea* spp.)

water poppy (*Hydrocleys nyphoides*)

yellow water iris (*Iris pseudacorus*)

Edging Plants for Ponds or Streams

astilbe (*Astilbe* spp.)

bee balm (*Monarda didyma*)

black snakeroot (*Cimicifuga racemosa*)

brunnera (*Brunnera macrophylla*)

cardinal flower (*Lobelia cardinalis*)

chameleon plant (*Houttuynia cordata*)

goatsbeard (*Aruncus dioicus*)

gooseneck loosestrife (*Lysimachia clethroides*)

Japanese iris (*Iris ensata*)

Japanese jack-in-the-pulpit (*Arisaema sikokiana*)

Japanese primrose (*Primula japonica*)

ligularia (*Ligularia* spp.)

masterwort (*Astrantia major*)

shining coneflower (*Rudbeckia nitida*)

swamp rose (*Rosa palustris*)

swamp sunflower (*Helianthus angustifolia*)

willow amsonia (*Amsonia tabernaemontana*)

yellow flag iris (*Iris pseudacorus*)

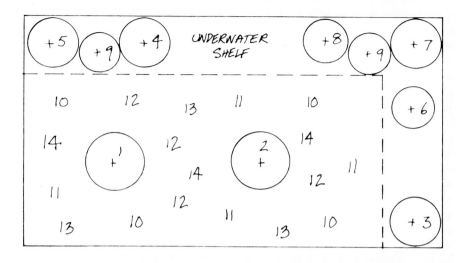

A WATER GARDEN

Plant List
(number of plants needed in parentheses)

1. Hardy water lily, *Nymphaea* 'Fabiola' (1)
2. Hardy water lily, *Nymphaea odorata* 'Sulfurex Grandiflora' (1)
3. Blue flag, *Iris versicolor* (1)
4. Siberian iris, *Iris sibirica* (2)
5. Yellow water iris, *Iris pseudacorus* (1)
6. Lizard's-tail, *Saururus cernuus* (1)
7. Common horsetail, *Equisetum byemale* (1)
8. Pickerel rush, *Poniederia cordata* (1)
9. Bogbean, *Menyanibes trifoliata* (2)
10. Anacharis, *Elodea canadensis* var. *gigantea* (4)
11. Awl-leaf arrowhead, *Sagittaria subulata* (4)
12. Water celery, *Vallisneria americana* (4)
13. Milfoil, *Myriophyllum aquaticum* (3)
14. Fanwort, *Cabomba caroliniana* (3)

PHOTOGRAPHY CREDITS

© CATHY WILKINSON BARASH: PP. 152, 166, 174, 178

© PHILIP BEAURLINE: PP. 150, 153, 175

© CRANDALL & CRANDALL PHOTOGRAPHY: PP. 11, 55, 164, 165, 177, 185, 211

© KEN DRUSE: PP. 39 BOTTOM, 241, 249, 267

ENVISION © BEN ASEN: P. 20, © NANCY S. DITURI: P. 54, © TIM GIBSON: P. 50, © JEAN HIGGINS: P. 12 BOTTOM RIGHT, © B.W. HOFFSMAN: PP. 14, 21, © WILLIAM MORIARTY: P. 75

© DEREK FELL: PP. 7, 18, 35, 46, 69, 74, 117, 129, 138, 180, 190 BOTTOM, 194, 197, 200, 203, 213, 221, 228, 236, 269, 283

© FULL FRAME PHOTOGRAPHY: P. 133

© JOHN GLOVER: PP. 19, 31, 42, 44, 45, 53, 60, 68, 75, 104, 107, 122 BOTH, 127 RIGHT, 136, 140, 142, 145, 169, 182, 218–219, 222 BOTTOM LEFT, 239, 243, 247, 251, 254, 263, 266 BOTH, 275

© MICK HALES: PP. 139, 229, 258–259, 282

© MARGARET HANSEL/POSITIVE IMAGES: P. 16

© NANCY HILL: PP. 29, 30, 33, 34, 39 TOP, 49, 65

© SAXON HOLT: PP. 27, 43, 186, 188, 222 TOP LEFT, 233

© BRUCE JENKINS/FULL FRAME PHOTO LIBRARY: PP. 37, 248, 261, 273, 280,

© JUDYWHITE: PP. 86, 89, 101 RIGHT, 119, 121, 123, 124 LEFT, 131, 137 TOP, 141, 144, 155, 159, 160, 163, 173, 176, 179 TOP, 190 TOP, 193, 195, 196, 198, 201, 204, 208

© DENCY KANE: PP. 106, 112 RIGHT, 115, 116 TOP, 143, 151, 162, 202

© LYNN KARLIN: PP. 28, 36, 213 LEFT

© MICHAEL LANDIS: PP. 187, 240, 244, 246, 250, 253, 260

LEO DE WYS © COMNET: P. 47, © J. MESSERSCHMIDT: P. 17

© DAVID LIVINGSTON: PP. 116 BOTTOM, 130, 132

© ROBERT E. LYONS: PP. 54, 70, 156, 199 TOP

© MARIANNE MAJERUS: PP. 56, 61, 63, 66, 252, 255, 279

© CHARLES MANN: PP. 25, 38, 48, 57 RIGHT, 78–79, 91, 100, 102, 111, 120, 124 RIGHT, 127 LEFT, 128, 134, 135, 148, 149, 161 BOTTOM, 167, 168, 170, 171, 181, 189, 191, 199 BOTTOM, 206, 207, 209, 210, 231, 234, 253, 264–265, 270 BOTH, 271, 274, 276 BOTTOM, 277 BOTH

© BRUCE MCCANDLESS: P. 26

© ELEANOR S. MORRIS: P. 12 TOP LEFT

NEW ENGLAND STOCK PHOTO © H. SCHMEISER: P. 51, © A. SCHWABEL: P. 59, © JOHN WELLS: PP. 15 RIGHT, 62, 223

© CLIVE NICHOLS: PP. 22, 23 (DESIGNER: SUE BERGER); 80, 85 (LOCATION: HADESPEN GARDENS, SOMERSET); 87, 90 (LOCATION: PYRFORD COURT, SURREY); 93 (LOCATION: HAZELBURY MANOR GARDEN, WILTSHIRE); 94 (LOCATION: THE OLD RECTORY, FARNBOROUGH, OXFORDSHIRE); 97 (DESIGNER: SUE BERGER); 99 (LOCATION: DAVID HICK'S GARDEN, OXFORDSHIRE); 101 LEFT (LOCATION: LOWER HOUSE FARM, GWENT, WALES); 103 (LOCATION: ASHTREE COTTAGE, WILTSHIRE); 108 (LOCATION: NATIONAL ASTHMA CAMPAIGN GARDEN); 114 (DESIGNER: ANTHONY NOEL); 118, 125 (LOCATION: LOWER HALL GARDEN, SHROPSHIRE); 157, 158, 183, 192, 212, 215, 224, 226, 230, 237, 262, 278

© MARIA PAPE/FPG INTERNATIONAL: P. 24

© SPENCER PARSHALL/DEMBINSKY PHOTO ASSOCIATES: P. 41

© JERRY PAVIA: PP. 67, 81, 82, 83, 84, 92, 96, 98, 105, 110, 112 LEFT, 123, 126, 161 TOP, 184, 220, 225 BOTH, 232, 238 BOTH, 272 BOTH

© JOANNE PAVIA: PP. 8–9, 52, 64, 109, 154, 172, 205, 214

PHOTO-NATS © GAY BUMGARNER: P. 32, © PRISCILLA CONNELL: P. 73, © JENNIFER GRAYLOCK: P. 13, © SYDNEY KARP: P. 10, 245

© WARREN SCHULTZ: P. 137 BOTTOM

© SHELLEY SECCOMBE: P. 40

© RICHARD SHIELL: P. 179 BOTTOM

© CAROL SPIER: P. 15 LEFT

© TIM STREET-PORTER: PP. 88 (ARCHITECTS: SMITH MILLER HAWKIN); 113

© CYNTHIA WOODYARD: PP. 57 LEFT, 71, 72, 227, 235, 242, 256, 268, 269 TOP RIGHT, 276, 281

Index